Rugmaking
& Macramé

Rugmaking & Macramé

A Step-by-Step Guide

**Noreen Gladwin
and Anna North**

Hamlyn
London · New York · Sydney · Toronto

Published by
The Hamlyn Publishing Group Ltd
London · New York · Sydney · Toronto
Astronaut House, Feltham, Middlesex, England
© Copyright The Hamlyn Publishing Group Ltd 1974
ISBN 600 361 020
Printed in England by Chapel River Press, Andover, Hants

Contents

Needle-made rug designs by Noreen Gladwin

Macramé designs by Anna North

An Introduction to Needle-Made Rugs

Rug-making is a creative hobby, ideal for those who enjoy a project which grows gradually, evening after evening. By starting with a small item such as a slipmat or a rug to cover a blanket box or old oak chest, the beginner can soon have the tremendous satisfaction of seeing a design take shape.

In the following chapters, you will find instructions for making smooth-faced and short pile rugs of lasting beauty. These are ideal for areas of medium wear and tear, such as sitting-rooms or bedrooms. Indeed, some of the finer work is so attractive that the rugs are never laid on the floor at all, but used as wallhangings.

There are two types of needle-made rugs, referred to as smooth-faced and pile rugs. In smooth-faced work, the stitches recommended for beginners are Cross-stitch, Long-legged Cross-stitch, Rice stitch and Interlocking Gobelin. The stitches used in pile rugs are Surrey stitch and Turkey or Ghiordes knot. These are all fully described and shown later in this section.

The Materials You Need

Canvas   Double mesh canvas is recommended to give greater strength. It can be obtained with 3, 4, 5, 7, 8, 9 and 10 holes to the inch, and even more, but these finer materials are not suggested for beginners. The most suitable canvas to begin with is 5 stitches to the inch. Choose a double mesh cotton canvas. Jute, the alternative, is more difficult to work as the weave is so much tighter and the holes are not easy to see.

You can obtain both single and double mesh canvas by the yard in any length and in widths between the selvedges varying from 12in to 48in. A width of 12in is ideal to start; the slipmats worked as our first examples are based on this. You should allow an extra $\frac{1}{4}$ yd of canvas for each design, for turning over at the ends and any necessary adjustments.

Although the canvas is described by the number of holes to the inch, it is actually the bars you count to determine the number of stitches. In double mesh canvas the warp and usually the weft threads, are arranged in 'double bars'. This means that they are in pairs of threads close together; the larger spaces between each pair form the significant holes.

Wool   It is important to use the best quality materials for needle-made rugs. In a craft where time and patience are involved, it is false economy to make do with second-best. There is no doubt that pure wool gives the best results; mixtures of wool and cotton or other fibres are never as satisfactory.

If you are in any doubt about the composition of a yarn, apply the burning test. Cut off a small strand and hold a lighted match underneath it. If the cut end smoulders, the yarn is all wool; if it burns, it contains other fibres. Needless to say, this is an experiment to conduct yourself, under controlled conditions, and not to delegate to a child.

There is, however, one way in which you can cut down considerably on the cost of wool, and that is by buying what are known as 'thrums'. These are the off-cuts from the carpet factories, the short lengths that are left over and of no further use on the large looms. Most useful in needle rugs are 2-ply Axminster thrums, which are generally recommended for use in double strands on 5-stitch canvas and single strands on 7-stitch canvas. The thrums are, of course, available in a wide range of attractive colours – picture all the colours that go into the making of Axminster carpets – and the cost varies according to the lengths of the cuts.

Since this is such an economical way of buying wool, it is well worth tracking down a source of supply. Most specialist needlecraft shops will sell bags of mixed thrums, and you can send for them by post to some carpet factories. Ask in your local craft shops; enquire of the needlecraft lecturer at an evening-class institute or of the crafts organiser of your local women's organisation.

In the UK, readers can order thrums by post from T. L. Winwood (Kidderminster) Carpets, PO Box 27, Lisle Avenue, Kidderminster, Worcestershire. Write to them for a price list for thrums, hanks and canvas, and for samples of the rug wool colours.

Readers in America and Canada will be able to obtain yarn from The Yarn Depot, 545 Sutter St, San Francisco, California 94102; Lily Mills Co, Dept HWH, Shelby, North Carolina 28150, or The Village Weaver, 8 Cumberland St, Toronto, Ontario, Canada.

It is not advisable to buy packages of wool in random mixed colours, since the chances are that you will receive one or two colours that will blend well with the schemes you have in mind but the others might seem never to fit in with anything.

Wool bought by the hank costs more, but you can save money by buying a large quantity in one or two good background colours, or in a selection of different shades of one colour, and then use thrums for the patterning.

The judgement of the exact thickness of wool to use is one of the arts of needle-made rug design. If you use too little wool you will produce a rug which is loose and lacks body, whereas too much wool distorts the shape and produces uneven bulges. The weight of wool required for both smooth-faced and pile rugs is generally about 6oz per square foot.

It is essential that the canvas is completely and evenly covered. To ensure this it is always advisable to work a small square sampler before starting on a design. Place the worked sample flat on a table, smooth it out and observe it critically for texture and appearance.

Adjustments in the tension can be made by working mainly with two strands but using one strand occasionally, or vice versa, carrying out the bulk of the work with wool in single strand and filling in with some in two strands. The working of a sampler has another advantage: it enables you to become familiar with the stitch and the relationship of the wool and the canvas before beginning the project.

Needles The needles for rugs should be large enough for the wool to be threaded easily through the eye, and should have blunt points. Generally (though one has to make allowance for personal preference) sizes 14–16 needles are used for 5-stitch canvas, and sizes 18–22 for 7-stitch canvas.

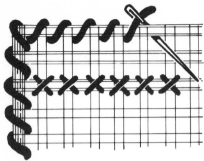

Fig. 1

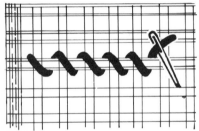

Fig. 2

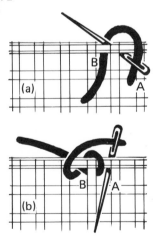

(a)

(b)

(c)

Preparation of Canvas

There should be 2–2½in turn-over at each end of the rug. One end can be firmly fixed with Cross-stitch (see Fig. 1) with needle and thread, not wool. The other end should be only temporarily secured by over-stitch until the work is almost completed (Fig. 2). This will prevent the second end from fraying during the course of the work, but allows for any necessary adjustment in the length of worked canvas, which does occasionally happen, however carefully one has counted the rows.

When the design is nearly finished, and the exact number of rows still to be worked has been accurately checked, the second edge can be adjusted, if need be, and securely sewn with a firm row of Cross-stitch. Each hole of the turned-over sections must lie exactly over the corresponding one beneath it; the rug is then worked through the double thickness of the canvas.

For pile rugs, the fold-over should be on the front face of the canvas. The little rough-cut edges are hidden by the pile. For smooth-faced rugs, the edging should be turned under, otherwise there will be a slight ridge at the rough-cut edges and the change from single to double thickness of canvas will show in the finished work. Even with a small piece of canvas being prepared for work as a sampler, the edges must be turned over to prevent fraying. Allow 1–1½in for these small working squares, and firmly oversew the edges.

The canvas must be doubled over in a particular way to ensure a neat and durable finish. This is shown in Fig. 1. As you can see, the canvas is folded between a double bar of weft threads so that these two threads form the extreme edge. If you fold the canvas so that the crease falls along a line of holes, the edge will have a castellated appearance and give a most unsatisfactory finish.

Edging Just as it is vital to allow a good turn-over at the ends of the rug and to secure them with firm Cross-stitches, so it is important to work a neat, even edging all round the canvas. Fig. 2 illustrates the three stages of the plaited edging stitch, which is simple to work and gives a strong, hard-wearing finish. To work this edging stitch on a piece of canvas for a pile rug, have the canvas with the cut edge facing upwards and start in the hole at the top right-hand corner. For a smooth-faced rug, have the canvas cut edge underneath.

Fig. 2a shows the first stage, the initial edging Cross-stitch. The wool is taken from back to front of the canvas through hole A, leaving a small end of wool about 2in long. This end is held at the top of the work with the free hand and will be covered by subsequent stitches. The needle passes to the left over the top of the canvas and through hole B again from back to front. This is the first half of the Cross-stitch.

In Fig. 2b the needle is shown passing over the top of the canvas again, back over the laid thread, and into hole A, once more from the back of the work. This completes the Cross-stitch.

Fig. 2c shows the 'on 3, back 2' stage of the stitch. The needle passes over hole B and is carried along a further 2 holes. It is taken through hole C, from back to front, and carried over the front of the work to pass through hole B once more, from the back.

With only a little practice you will find that this stitch comes very easily. It is as well to be able to work it neatly and evenly before starting a full-size rug. Remember that the wool always passes from the back to the front of the canvas: it is always carried forward 3 stitches and back 2 stitches; that is to say, missing 2 holes on the forward stitch and 1 on the backward stitch.

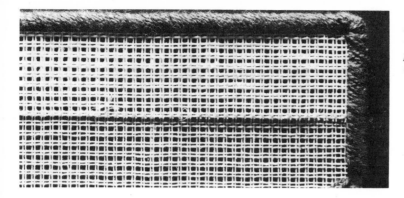

The edging is always worked in the main background colour of the rug, or of the border, and usually in three strands of the wool. The corners are particularly difficult to cover, however carefully you work. To avoid any unsightly show-through of the light-coloured canvas, it is advisable, especially for beginners, to put a thick dab of paint from a child's paint box on the corners. Alternatively, use crayons, choosing a colour as near as possible to that of the wool.

Another way is to oversew the corners and about $\frac{1}{2}$in either side with a single strand of the wool. Do not despair if the corners lack a professional finish at first. Most people have to work at least ten corners before achieving a perfect one.

Continue working the edging stitch along the top edge of the turned-over canvas. When you reach the corner, gradually diminish the length of the plait. Make a stitch over 3 holes forward, 2 holes back until just before the corner; then 2 forward, 1 back; then 1 forward. This will make the last stitch in the row a simple Cross-stitch. Make the first stitch along the selvedge in the same way, beginning with a Cross-stitch, then 2 forward, 1 back, then 3 forward and 2 back and so on.

Work the edging stitch for 2in down the left-hand selvedge, then leave it. Return to the top right-hand corner and work the corner as described, and continue the edging stitch for 2in down that selvedge. Leave it there. The picture above shows the stitch at this stage.

With smooth-faced rugs, the edging is not returned to until the work is otherwise completed; then the edging stitch is continued right round the work. With pile rugs, the edging is worked about 2in ahead of the knotting, and so you put in a little more edging, work some more rows of knotting and so on.

When coming to the end of a strand of wool, always finish at hole C. Thread more wool into the needle, slip through the back of the plait which has been worked, bring out at hole C and then go back to hole B. Continue with the new length of wool, holding the short end of the original strand along the top so that it is bound behind the top canvas bar (see Fig. 2c).

Smooth-faced rugs are worked from left to right and down the canvas; pile rugs from left to right up the canvas.

For the beginner, it is usually essential to start by copying designs, at least until confidence in the general principles of needle-made rugs has been gained. The designs that follow are all worked from charts, one square representing one stitch.

Any pattern which is charted on squares is suitable for adaptation, and there are countless books and leaflets giving designs for Cross-stitch embroidery or Fair Isle knitting which are ideal. It is important to master the art of reading a design from a chart and to work simply by counting stitches. You should never need to mark the design on the canvas.

The border of a rug, to give the correct 'feel', should occupy about one-sixth of the total area. It can be more, according to the design, but should never be less. Outlines of a design should be worked in a dark colour to tone with the background of the rug – brown or navy blue, perhaps, but never black. This gives too harsh a contrast. It is advisable always to work from the dark to the lighter colours of a design.

As you become more interested in adapting designs or creating your own, you might like to copy some designers who take a notebook of squared paper round with them and use it as a sketchbook, drawing in any pattern they see on an Oriental rug in a shop or museum, from a piece of knitting or embroidery, or sketching from life. Fig. 3 shows this at its very simplest: a leaf shape 'squared up' to form part of a design.

Completed rugs should never be lined. Some beginners think that by doing so they extend the life of their handwork, but this is not the case. Grit and dirt will work between the face of the rug and backing and, with constant wear, will agitate the threads and eventually possibly cut the wool. With a good quality canvas and the correct weight of wool, your rugs should live happily ever after.

One great advantage of needle-made rugs is that in the case of bad patches of wear, repairs can easily be made. For this reason, it is sensible to hoard all the left-over lengths of wool so that you can always match the colour at a later stage.

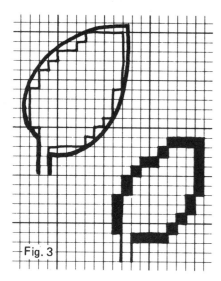

Fig. 3

The Basic Stitches

Smooth-faced designs

It is always comforting, when embarking on a new craft, to find certain basic elements which are familiar and simple. In needle-made rugs, one of those elements is the extensive use of Cross-stitch. Most people know that it consists of two stitches of equal length, crossing each other at right angles.

To work Cross-stitch in smooth-faced rug work, the two stitches forming the cross slope across an intersection of two bars of canvas. The top of the cross should always run from bottom left to top right. It is important to be consistent about this, and never to work some of the stitches with the uppermost thread running in the opposite direction. A most untidy appearance will result.

The quickest way to work a large area of Cross-stitches is to work a row of stitches all going in one direction, and then to work back along the row with the stitches at right angles.

This practice is acceptable where large areas of background are being worked, but is not generally recommended. It has been found that a far more satisfactory covering of the canvas, and a firmer fabric, is achieved when the stitches are worked separately, that is, when each stitch is completed before the next one is begun.

If this method of working stitches still does not result in complete covering of the canvas, it is possible to lay a single strand of wool over a double weft bar, from left to right, and work the Cross-stitches over it. Fig. 1 shows the working of a Cross-stitch in detail.

The thread enters the canvas, from the back, in hole A, is taken over the canvas diagonally, from right to left, into hole B. It then travels behind the canvas vertically down into hole C, and over the canvas, diagonally from left to right, into hole D; the thread enters hole C again and is taken diagonally to the left.

The sampler in the picture on page 12 is worked in Cross-stitch. As you can see, the outline and numbers are worked first.

Long-legged Cross-stitch

This stitch resembles a flat version of the plaited edging stitch shown on page 8. The difference is that instead of the plait proceeding on 3 holes, back 2 holes, it travels 2 holes forward and 1 hole back. The row of stitches always starts and finishes with a Cross-stitch.

The stitch is very economical in the use of wool and, because of its closely interlocking nature, gives a particularly hard-wearing fabric; it has the appearance of herringbone lines. It can be worked in straight lines from right to left, left to right, and vertically in either direction. A very attractive effect is achieved by working the stitch in different

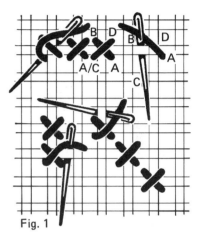

Fig. 1

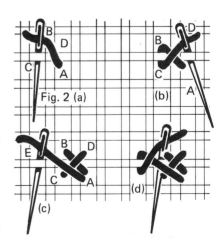

Fig. 2 (a)   (b)

(c)   (d)

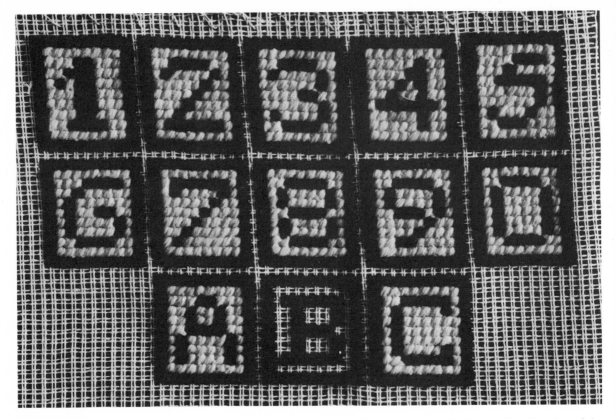

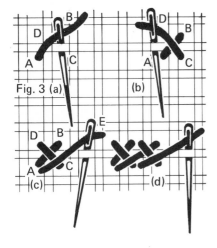

Fig. 3 (a) (b)

(c) (d)

The simple number and alphabet sampler, worked in Cross-stitch, shows how easy it is to adapt curved and circular shapes to the limitations of the stitch.

directions on one piece of work. To do this, change the direction of the stitch, not the canvas.

To begin the stitch, make an ordinary Cross-stitch, with the lower half of the stitch worked in the direction in which the plait is to travel. To work the stitch from right to left (Fig. 2), the needle is inserted in the canvas from the back, at hole A.

The thread travels diagonally to the left into hole B, behind the canvas vertically down into hole C and diagonally upwards to the right into hole D. This completes the first Cross-stitch. The thread is then taken behind the work and into the back of hole A again, then over the work diagonally to the left over 2 holes, into hole E. Another Cross-stitch is made with the thread finishing in hole C again.

Fig. 3 illustrates the working of this stitch from left to right.

This stitch is often worked between the edging stitch and the start of the pile in pile rugs; it not only supports the pile, but also adds to the durability of the work.

The Christmas tree pattern shown in the picture on page 13 is a small sampler of Long-legged Cross-stitch worked in three colours. The chart given beside it shows how this simple pattern is built up. It can easily be incorporated into a design for slipmats or small rugs.

Deep Long-legged Cross-stitch is a variety of the stitch, worked over two double bars. Thus, it doubles the width covered by a single row of stitches. Its use adds interest to a rug by providing a texture contrast, yet without altering the general overall appearance.

Fig. 4 shows the working of the stitch in detail, in this case in a row from right to left. As can be seen, the thread travels vertically behind the canvas and diagonally across the face.

Rice Stitch

This stitch is formed of a large cross to start with, then all four corners are crossed in turn by a small diagonal stitch, which ties down the arms, as it were.

Fig. 5 shows in detail how it is worked from right to left, with the large cross being made using holes A, B, C and D over a diagonal in each direction of three stitches. The small tying corner stitches are made in this order: top right-hand corner, bottom right-hand corner, top left-hand corner, and bottom left-hand corner. The thread then returns to hole 3, ready to travel diagonally to the left again to make the next large Cross-stitch.

The stitch produces a very hard-wearing fabric but is rather extravagant in its use of wool. If any difficulty is encountered in adequate covering of the canvas, a row of Back-stitches can be worked between each row of stitches. However, this can be avoided by working Rice-stitch in conjunction with another stitch, such as Cross-stitch or Long-legged Cross-stitch, which have better covering capacity.

The sample shown in the picture on page 15 is worked in a combination of Long-legged stitch, used for the rust-coloured background and the blue pattern, with four blocks of Rice-stitch in white. The small chart opposite the picture gives the stitch count in detail.

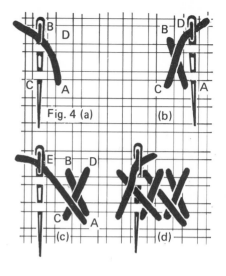

Interlocking Gobelin Stitch

As the picture on page 14 shows, this stitch is ideal for a striped pattern, since it is worked in horizontal rows backwards and forwards. It is also highly suitable for a beginner since it is not only another slight variation of Cross-stitch, and therefore not entirely unfamiliar, but the

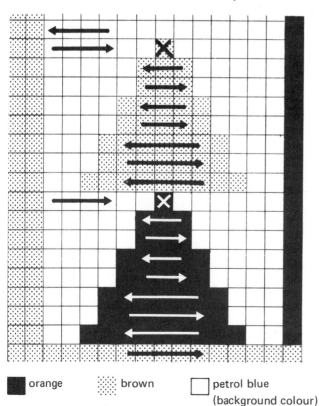

■ orange ▒ brown □ petrol blue (background colour)

Long-legged Cross-stitch worked in three colours. The double triangle pattern represents a Christmas tree.

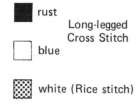

■ rust
         Long-legged
         Cross Stitch

□ blue

▧ white (Rice stitch)

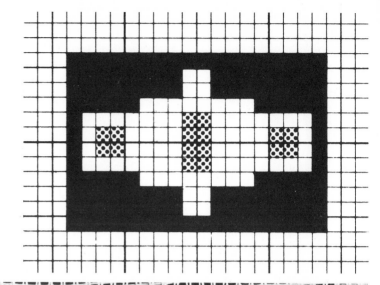

Interlocking Gobelin stitch worked in horizontal stripes in three colours.

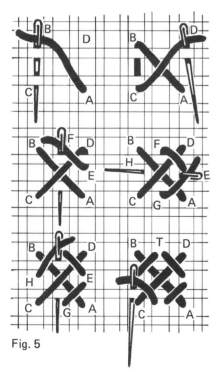

Fig. 5

work progresses very quickly. The first row of stitches is like a row of the first half of Cross-stitches, but worked over one double bar, horizontally.

At the end of a row, the last stitch drops down an extra hole and the stitch is then completed, travelling back in the opposite direction. In order to cover the canvas completely, the first stitch of the first row and the last stitch of the last row should be finished with half a Cross-stitch.

The colours used in our sampler, from the outside, are deep coral, rust, white, and a centre row of blue. They were chosen to illustrate the effectiveness of the stitch, whether worked in a sharp contrast – the blue and white next to each other – or in harmonising colours – the coral and rust.

Fig. 6 shows the working of the stitch in detail; you can see that the bottom half of the first row of stitches is crossed by the next row. Again, the thread travels vertically at the back of the canvas and diagonally on the face.

14

Clearer definition is achieved when the same design is worked in Long-legged Cross-stitch and, for the white sections, Rice-stitch.

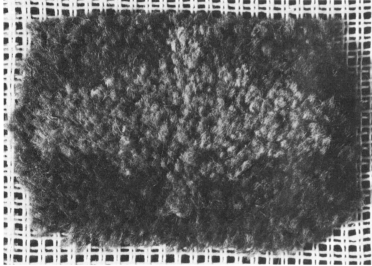

Surrey stitch in a diamond pattern. The short-pile stitch softens the outlines of the design.

Short Pile Designs

As has already been explained, pile rugs are worked with the turn-over cut edge of the canvas uppermost. The work is held with the length of the canvas away from the worker, whereas in smooth-faced designs the work is held with the full length of the canvas coming towards the worker.

Surrey Stitch

Each stitch in this work covers the canvas in two directions, both vertically and horizontally, and so forms an especially hard-wearing rug. Each knot requires two movements of the needle, the first one towards the worker and the second from right to left at right angles to the first. In this way, the needle passes through each hole four times.

The pictures above show how adaptable charted designs can be: this is the same pattern, in the top sampler, worked in Long-legged Cross-stitch and Rice-stitch and, below that, in Surrey Stitch.

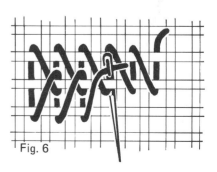

Fig. 6

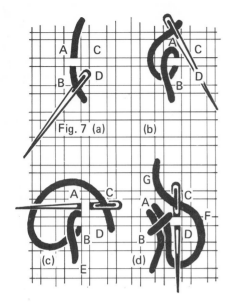

Fig. 7 (a)   (b)

(c)   E   (d)

If you follow the working diagrams of Fig. 7, a to d, you will soon find that you can work the stitch almost as a reflex action. To help simplify the working of the stitch, think of it as consisting of two blanket stitches. The one that is worked towards you is not pulled tight. The horizontal stitch is.

Begin by inserting the needle under a double weft bar, towards you, from hole A to hole B. Draw the wool through until slightly more than the required length of the pile is left (Fig. 7a). In 5-stitch canvas, on which our samples are worked, this will be $\frac{3}{4}$in. Carry the needle to the left of this short end and bring the short end straight down over the bar (Fig. 7b), holding it firmly in place with the thumb, just below where the stitch is being worked.

Insert the needle again at hole C and bring it out at hole A, passing it over the loop of wool (Fig. 7c). Draw the needle down and pull it towards you, making a knot on top of the canvas. Cut the wool to the length of the pile – $\frac{3}{4}$in in this case – if the next stitch is to be worked in a different colour.

If you are continuing with the same wool, take the needle under the canvas, between holes C and D and through the loop (Fig. 7d). Draw the needle through until the loop is the length of the pile. Hold the loop down firmly with the left thumb below the stitch, as before. Take the thread upwards, as in Fig. 7b, and complete the stitch by taking the thread through hole F and then hole C, horizontally, as before. Continue along the row, making loops as described, until a change of colour is needed. When it is, cut the wool to the length of the pile, as described above.

Turkey or Ghiordes Knot

This knot is worked over the two threads forming the double bar of the warp on double mesh canvas, and not only through the larger spaces, usually referred to simply as the 'holes' in the canvas.

In single mesh canvas, the Turkey or Ghiordes knot is worked over the warp threads in pairs. Unlike Surrey-stitch, it is worked in one direction only and so produces a less hard-wearing fabric, though the two types of knots are indistinguishable on the face of the work. It is possible, however, to tell which method has been used from the reverse. Both give a neat finish and a faithful reproduction of the pattern on the reverse of the canvas, but Surrey-stitch is perhaps more attractive to look at since it provides greater coverage of the backing.

Compare the reverse sides of the two methods in the pictures opposite. The rectangular block, on the right, is the reverse of the sampler of Surrey-stitch and the L-shaped block is Turkey knot. You can see the Turkey knot sampler, right way up, in the picture on page 18 and follow it, stitch by stitch, using the accompanying chart.

Follow Fig. 8 a to d for the working details of the knot on double mesh canvas. Insert the needle behind a left-hand bar of the canvas (A) and out (B) to the face of the canvas (Fig. 8a), holding down a short end of the wool with the left thumb.

Take the needle across the front of both bars, behind the right-hand one (C) and out again in the space (B) between them (Fig. 8b). Pull the knot tight (Fig. 8c).

Unless a new colour is to be used for the next stitch (in which case cut the loop for the length of pile required, as in Surrey-stitch) proceed along the row, making loops across each pair of double warp bars in the row (Fig. 8d).

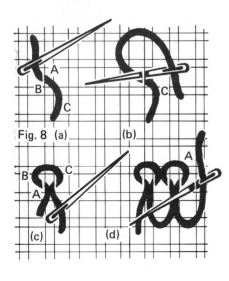

Fig. 8 (a)   (b)

(c)   (d)

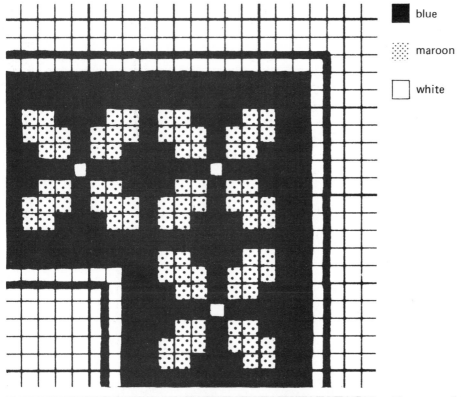

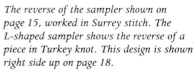 blue

▒ maroon

□ white

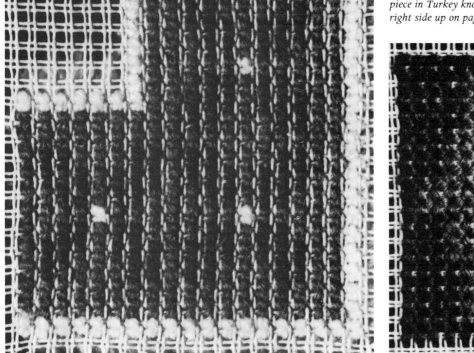

The reverse of the sampler shown on page 15, worked in Surrey stitch. The L-shaped sampler shows the reverse of a piece in Turkey knot. This design is shown right side up on page 18.

*A corner worked in a short-pile stitch,
Turkey (or Ghiordes) knot. This stitch is
worked in one direction only.*

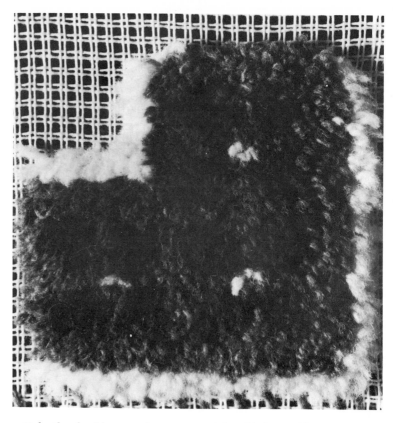

Only the double warp bars are used for this knot. The next row is
worked on the row of double warp bars above. In both Surrey-stitch
and Ghiordes or Turkey knot, it is advisable to cut the pile at the end
of each row. Before you are experienced at the work, it is better to
make the loops slightly longer than the required length of pile so that
if there is any unevenness the cut ends can be trimmed without making
the pile shorter than planned.

However carefully the loops are cut, the pile will almost certainly
need trimming. To do this, place the work flat on a table, push the pile
gently away from you a row at a time, and trim with a good pair of
sharp scissors. The look of the pile is further improved if it is 'combed'
with the fingers – that is, scrabbled slightly to remove loose ends and
bits of fluff.

Something to Show For It

Now that you have learned a selection of stitches and knots, you can start putting them into practice by making small rugs for the home. To begin with, it is easiest to follow the charted designs in the stitches given for each rug. In this way, you can check that your tension is giving you the correct measurements as quoted, and that your work looks like the patterns in the pictures.

Later, when you have a little more experience, you can take a chart for a design in one stitch and work another, to give you quite a different effect. Remember, too, what a vast difference you can make to the look of a rug simply by reversing the colours and using dark where we have used light, and vice versa.

Olive Green and Yellow Slipmat

Shown in colour on page 45.
Stitches
Cross-stitch and Long-legged Cross-stitch.

Measurements
The finished slipmat measures 12in by 26in.

Materials
1yd double-mesh canvas, 5 stitches to the inch, 12in wide; of 2-ply rug wool, or thrums, 1lb olive green; $\frac{1}{2}$lb yellow-green; No. 14 blunt-ended rug needle.

Method
The rug is worked with the olive green wool for the edging stitch, and the background and the design in yellow-green. The three boxes forming the pattern in the paler colour are worked in Cross-stitch and the remainder of the fabric in Long-legged Cross-stitch. However, the design could be worked entirely in Cross-stitch if preferred.

Turn over one end of the canvas 2–2$\frac{1}{2}$in and tie down securely with Cross-stitches worked with strong thread, as already described. Measure 26in from the fold and turn over at the other end. Trim the canvas to leave a 2–2$\frac{1}{2}$in fold. Secure this second turned-over end with over-stitch. Work edging stitch from right to left across the top.

Turn the corner with edging stitch – first colouring the canvas with paint or crayon in olive green, if desired – and continue the edging stitches for 2in down the left-hand side.

Work the top right-hand corner and continue edging stitch down right-hand side for 2in. Then leave the edging stitch to be completed when the mat is finished.

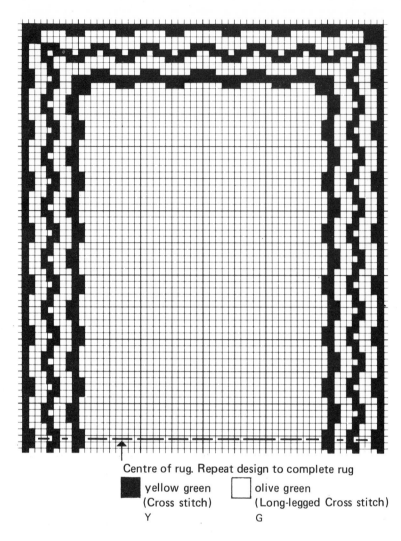

Centre of rug. Repeat design to complete rug

■ yellow green
  (Cross stitch)
  Y

□ olive green
  (Long-legged Cross stitch)
  G

Now start working the design. Work a line of Cross-stitch in yellow-green immediately under the edging stitch, across the mat from right to left. (The colours will be referred to as G, olive green; Y, yellow-green): 3 Cross-stitch Y; 4 Long-legged Cross-stitch G; 3 Cross-stitch Y; 5 Long-legged G; 3 Cross-stitch Y; 5 Long-legged G; 3 Cross-stitch Y; 5 Long-legged G; 3 Cross-stitch Y; 5 Long-legged G; 3 Cross-stitch Y; 5 Long-legged G; 3 Cross-stitch Y; 4 Long-legged G; 3 Cross-stitch Y. **Next row:** Work 3 Cross-stitches in Y; continue along row in Long-legged G; 3 Cross-stitches Y. This completes the first 2 rows of the design..Compare the written instructions with the chart, and continue following the design by reading the chart. Put in the design in Y in Cross-stitch and the background in G in Long-legged Cross-stitch.

Just before you reach the cut, turned-over hem of the canvas at the end of the work, count the number of rows left in the design and the number of rows in the canvas to the fold. Make any necessary adjustments by undoing the line of overstitching and refolding the canvas. When it is accurate, secure the canvas by a row of Cross-stitch with strong thread. Complete the design and then complete the edging stitch, neatly threading in the ends at the back of the work.

Purple Rya rug (see page 26)

Off-white and Pink Rug

Stitches
Cross-stitch and Long-legged Cross-stitch.

Measurements
The finished rug measures 18in (89 stitches) by 26in (123 stitches).

Materials
1 yd double-mesh canvas, 5 stitches to the inch, 18in wide; of 2-ply rug wool or thrums, 1lb off-white; $\frac{1}{2}$lb deep pink; No. 14–16 blunt-ended rug needle.

Method
The rug is worked with the off-white wool as the background colour, in Long-legged Cross-stitch in varying directions, and pink wool for the diamond patterning, in Cross-stitch.

Turn over one end of the canvas 2–2$\frac{1}{2}$in and secure as usual with Cross-stitch. See that the ends of the canvas face downwards, before starting the edging stitch. Work the plaited edging across width, then the top left-hand corner and 2in down the left-hand side. Returning to the right-hand side, work the corner and 2in down the right-hand side.

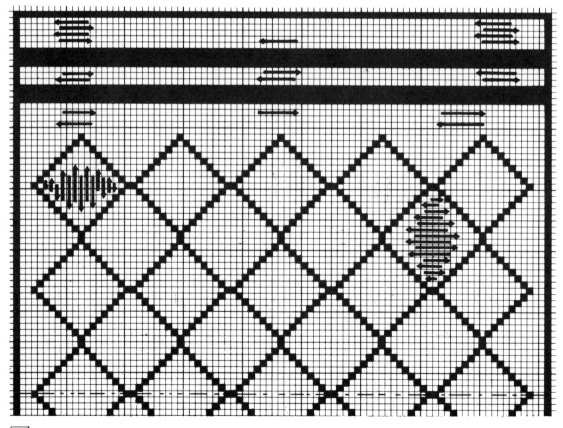

☐ off-white

■ pink

—·— Marks centre of design. Repeat to complete rug.

22

Leave the edging stitch and complete when the rug is otherwise finished.

In Long-legged Cross-stitch, work 5 rows in off-white wool; 3 rows pink; 3 off-white; 3 pink; 5 off-white – 19 rows in all.

Next row: Work 10 stitches in Long-legged Cross-stitch in off-white; 1 pink Cross-stitch, which gives the start of the diamond design. From this point, the diamond design in Cross-stitch is worked in advance of the background. Follow the chart stitch by stitch for the detail.

Note the interesting effect achieved by the use of different directions of the Long-legged Cross-stitch. This is indicated by the arrows on the chart. The first row of diamonds is filled in with vertical stitches, the next with horizontal, and so on.

When the diamond patterns have been completely filled in, you are ready to complete the striped end border of the rug, the last 19 rows.

Check the accuracy of the turned-over canvas and adjust if necessary; secure with Cross-stitch in thread.

In Long-legged Cross-stitch, work 5 rows in off-white; 3 pink; 3 off-white, 5 pink and 5 off-white. Finish off the edging plait round the rug.

This design is easily adapted to working on 22 or 27in canvas, and can be made in any combination of colours, either closely relating or contrasting. The whole fabric can be worked in Cross-stitch, but the effect will be less attractive.

The diamond pattern, in dark pink, is worked in Cross-stitch and the off-white background in Long-legged Cross-stitch in two directions, vertical and horizontal.

Cross-stitch Alphabet Sampler

Stitches
Cross-stitch.

Measurements
As shown in the picture on page 29, $10\frac{1}{2}$in by $14\frac{1}{2}$in.

Materials
$\frac{5}{8}$yd of double-mesh canvas, 5 stitches to the inch, 12in wide; oddments of 2-ply rug wool thrums in two colours; No. 14–16 blunt-ended wool needle.

Method
Each panel consists of 10 Cross-stitches in outline colour across the top and bottom and 11 stitches down each side. The accompanying chart shows how the letters have been adapted to Cross-stitch work. These are worked in the outline colour.

When the panels and letters are completed, fill in the background in the second colour. If desired, the vacant squares in the bottom row can be utilised to work the date when the panel was made, or the worker's initials.

A chart for the numerals is given on page 26. The sampler in picture, page 29, is worked in nylon yarn, which gives less 'body' to the panel but has the advantage of being washable. It could be enlarged for use as a nursery rug. To complete the panel, you can work the border in Long-legged Cross-stitch or continue in Cross-stitch. As a wall decoration, the panel can be framed or hung on a thin dowel.

□ brown

■ blue

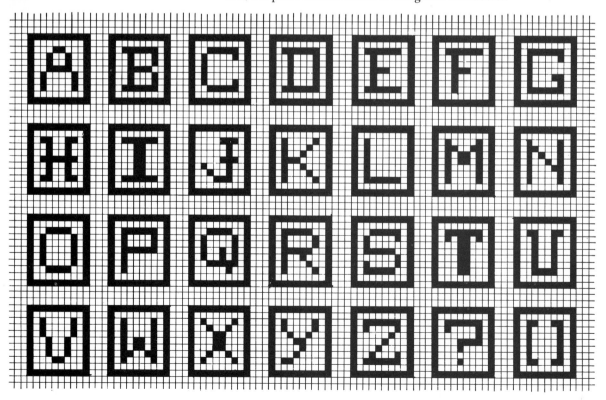

Geometric design in Turkey Knot (see page 27)

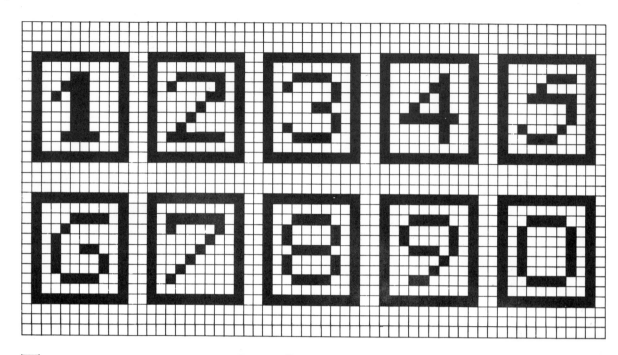

□ pink

■ brown

A sampler can be worked in numerals or the alphabet or both (see page 24).

Purple Rya Rug

Rya rugs imported from Scandinavia make colourful displays and, even though they tend to be rather expensive, are temptingly luxurious because of the length of their shaggy pile. Rugs of this type are simple to make in Surrey-stitch separated by Long-legged Cross-stitch.

Stitches
Surrey-stitch and Long-legged Cross-stitch.

Measurements
From edge to edge of the canvas, the rug measures 27in by 52in.

Materials
$1\frac{3}{4}$yd of double-mesh, 27in wide canvas, 5 stitches to the inch; No. 14–16 blunt-ended needle; allowing for a $2\frac{1}{2}$in pile, you will need approximately 10–12oz of 2-ply Axminster thrums per sq ft. Therefore, allow a total of about $10\frac{1}{2}$lb of wool.

The rug in the picture uses a mixture of only three colours – though the way they are blended gives the impression that there are more. The best effects are achieved with colour mixes that blend rather than contrast – purple, magenta and dark turquoise was our choice; shades of pink and red, of green and blue or orange and brown would look equally well.

Method
Fold over $2–2\frac{1}{2}$in of canvas at one end and secure with a row of Cross-stitch. Measure the length of the rug, plus a turn-over allowance at the other end. Cut the canvas, turn over the surplus and temporarily secure it with over-stitch. With the cut edge and the cross-stitching facing upwards, and using purple wool, begin the plaited edging stitch, as described.

Work 3 rows of purple Long-legged stitch before commencing the pile. This stitch worked at each end will give a firmer edge to the rug and protect the pile. Remember that you work Surrey-stitch by commencing in the bottom left-hand corner with the length of the canvas held away from you. Roll up the canvas as the work proceeds.

Follow the colour picture on page 21 for the general effect of the colour blending. For this type of random design, there is no chart. The pile commences with one strand each of the purple and magenta wools used together. As you can see, there are patches of magenta and purple used alone, and purple and turquoise worked together.

Work 2 rows of Long-legged Cross-stitch between each pile row. Where a pile row is continued in one colour, or one combination of two colours, complete the row before cutting the pile. Where the colour changes in the course of the row, cut off the end of one colour to the length of the pile and begin with another colour.

If it is found that the 2 rows of Long-legged Cross-stitch do not adequately cover the canvas, a row of Back-stitch in purple can be worked over the canvas bars, between the rows.

When you reach the turned-over 'hem' at the end of the rug, secure it with Cross-stitch (unless you have decided to make adjustments to the length) and work over the two thicknesses.

Work 3 rows of Long-legged Cross-stitch after the last pile row. Complete the edging stitch in purple.

The pile is pulled in opposite directions on the face of this Rya rug to show the two rows of Long-legged Cross-stitch worked between each pile row.

Geometric Design in Turkey Knot

A most striking colour combination ranging from dark chestnut brown to pale aubergine gives this rug, shown in colour on page 25, all the warmth and glow of a fireside on a winter's day. The pattern is made up of rectangles and interlocking shapes in four colours used singly and blended together.

Stitches
Turkey knot and Long-legged Cross-stitch.

Measurements
The rug measures 21in by 30in.

Material
1yd of double-mesh canvas, 5 stitches to the inch, 21in wide; of 2-ply Axminster thrums, a total of 2lb in 4 different, but harmonising colours.

Method
Prepare the canvas as usual and work the edging stitch to the point where it is left. Work 1 row of Long-legged Cross-stitch before commencing the first row in Turkey knot. In this case, the pile is $\frac{1}{2}$in long.

The design is not charted; if you are not going to follow it closely from the picture it is advisable to sketch out a rough idea of your own design, so you can check that it balances well as far as shape and distribution of colour are concerned.

You will notice that the 'background' colour of the rug changes in the centre. This means, of course, that the edging stitch is worked in the appropriate colour and that the last row of Long-legged stitch is worked in the second background colour.

Becoming Your Own Designer

As you can see from some of the examples given in detail, very effective designs can be made by working a simple geometric border on an otherwise plain background. So that you can adapt this type of design to the measurements you require, we are giving a number of charts for simple border patterns. These can, of course, be worked in a number of different stitches; probably by now you have one or two favourite ones with which you feel most confident.

First, a *Corner worked in Surrey stitch*, in deep red, dark brown and olive green. The brown outlines the green designs and gives more definition and clarity to the pattern. This pattern is suitable for use with 27in canvas, five stitches to the inch, though you can, of course, adapt it to practically any size.

You can work the large corner motifs at the four corners only or, on a larger piece of work, could repeat them in the centre of each of the two long sides. This pattern can be worked in Cross-stitch and Long-legged Cross-stitch, too; see how much firmer the outline is on the smooth-faced sample.

In the photograph on page 30 the corner is worked in Surrey stitch. On the right the motifs are repeated in Cross-stitch and Long-legged Cross-stitch. Follow the chart below whether you want to copy the design in a short-pile or smooth-faced stitch.

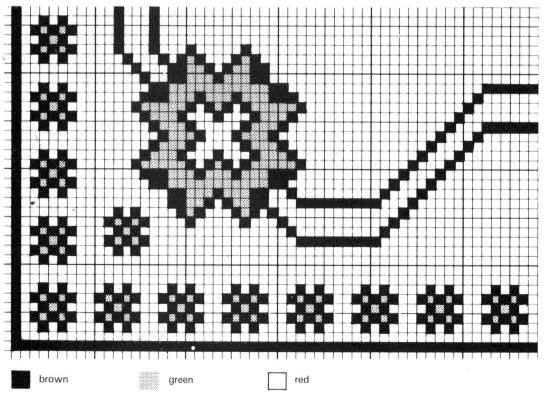

■ brown   ▦ green   ☐ red

Top: *Necklace and bracelet set (see page 60)*
Bottom: *Cross-stitch alphabet sampler (see page 24)*

Corner worked in Turkey knot (below and opposite)
Suitable for 27in-wide canvas, 5 stitches to the inch, this design is
worked in Turkey knot. If a smooth-faced rug is wanted, the design
can be adapted in Cross-stitch and Long-legged Cross-stitch. In the
latter case, the colours – deep maroon red and off-white – appear more
sharply in contrast, and the design bolder.

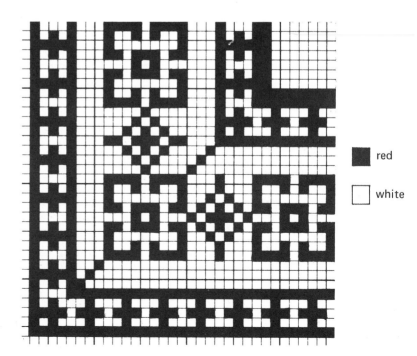

■ red

□ white

Corners in Long-legged Cross-stitch (below and on page 32)
Suitable for a slipmat worked on 12in-wide canvas, 5 stitches to the
inch, these designs are shown in Long-legged Cross-stitch, but can be
worked in Turkey knot or Surrey-stitch. Stripes in geometric patterns
can be worked inside the border design or omitted, as required.

As shown, the pattern on the left is worked in dark rust brown on a
dusty pink background, and the one on the right, in dark turquoise
blue on off-white. The small motif samples worked inside the border of
this design show the different effect obtained when two strong colours
are used instead of a dark and a light one together.

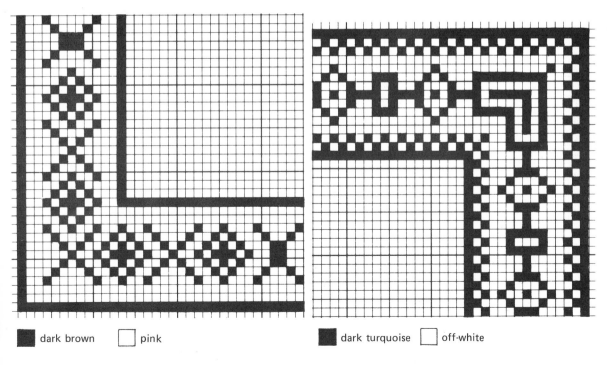

■ dark brown ☐ pink   ■ dark turquoise ☐ off-white

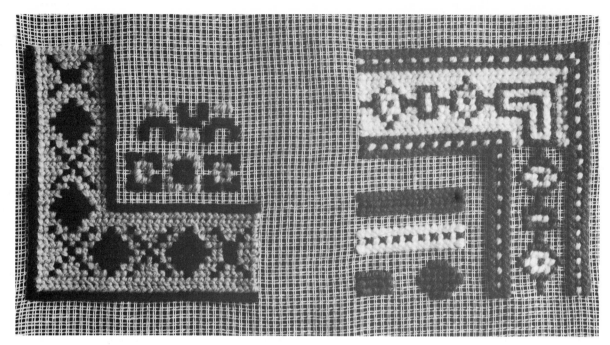

*Corners in Long-legged Cross-stitch
(see page 31).*

Six Geometric Motifs

The geometric motifs shown on the chart are suitable for working singly or in groups at the corner of a rug, or in stripes between two parallel lines to form a border. They can, of course, be enlarged in scale – making the outline two squares thick where it is one, and three where it is two – for larger pieces of work. As shown, the size is not really suitable for pieces larger than slipmats (see photograph on page 34).

Sisal rug (see page 57)

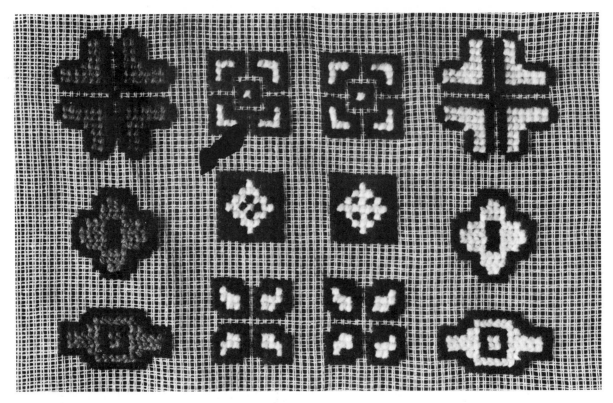

Geometric motifs (see chart on page 32).

Nursery Motifs

Where a simple border is worked on a nursery rug, a pattern of animal or toy motifs can be worked in the centre. The examples show boy and girl dolls dancing; a rabbit; a hen pecking; children with a dog and a large doll, trees and a motor car, and trees and lambs. This type of pattern can easily be adapted from drawings in children's painting books. You can square them up for needle work by following the method shown for adapting a leaf.

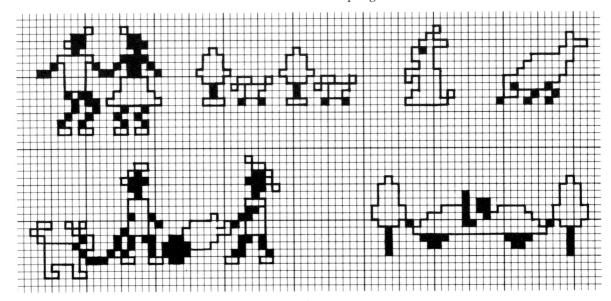

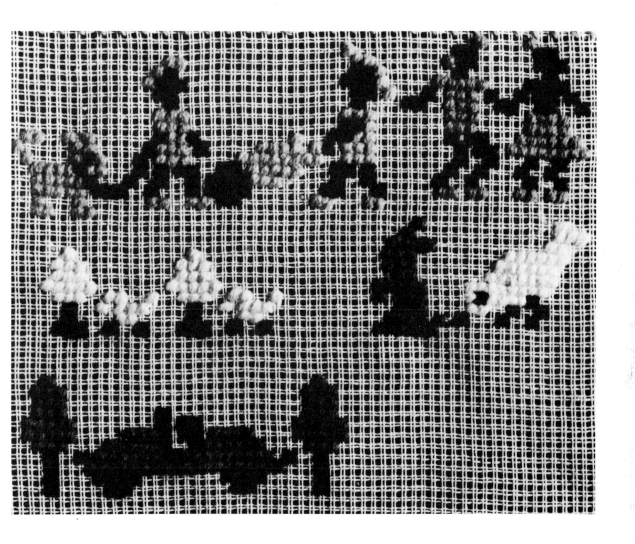

Macramé and bead door curtain (see pages 51 & 72)

Macramé

The Materials You will Need for Macramé

Anyone who can tie a knot can do macramé. This probably explains the enthusiastic revival of the craft, which had not been widely popular for nearly a hundred years. With today's demand for immediate success, instant results and high job satisfaction, macramé can't lose. For it is basically a form of making patterns by using only two types of knots, both of which are reasonably familiar in everyday life.

The first of these knots is called a Flat knot in macramé, but is exactly the same as a reef knot, the pride and joy of most schoolchildren who quickly master the art of tying it. Worked over two stationary vertical cords, (Fig. 1), this knot makes a braid that can form part of a door curtain, a wallhanging or can make a tie belt.

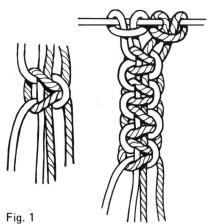

Fig. 1

You see, even the first basic stitches that a beginner practises can be put to use. This is what is so encouraging. Tiny samples of stitch patterns can be mounted on a fabric ground and make a decorative and memorable keep-sake – indeed, they have all the delight of early needle-work samplers and there is a charming example in a London museum.

The other basic stitch is called the Double Half-Hitch, which can be worked vertically, horizontally or diagonally, (Fig. 2), opening up endless pattern possibilities. This knot makes a corded effect and is often tied, albeit unwittingly, by people fastening off the ends when tying up parcels, for example.

No special outlay on equipment is necessary before you start macramé. The basic requirements, beyond the cord or twine itself, are pieces of board, thick cardboard, plastic foam sheeting, an old cushion or a clipboard to use as a working surface, glass-headed dressmaking pins, a crochet hook, knitting needle, a blunt-pointed wool needle with a large eye, loose-cover (T-shaped) pins, clear adhesive, rubber bands, a ruler, pencil, tape measure, scissors and possibly a C-clamp. You will probably have some of these round the home anyway (see Fig. 3).

The choice of yarn is all-important, because the weight and thickness determines the size and shape of the article you will make. But when you are practising at first, of course, you can work with whatever comes to hand, or whatever gives you most confidence. A sudden impulse to start macramé can quickly be satisfied by working with some twine that you will already have in the kitchen, the workroom or the tool shed, for there can scarcely be a household without the means of tying up a joint, a package or a row of runner beans.

You can use any yarn that is strong enough to withstand the action of knotting (which imposes quite a strain on the fibres) and able to be pulled into a tight knot without slipping. This means that the very slippery, shiny yarns are generally not suitable, and among these are a number of the synthetics. Yarns with too much 'give' in them, that are too elastic, tend to give problems, too, not only in working but in

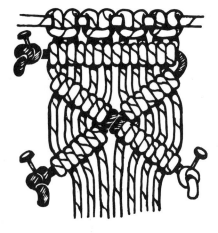

Fig. 2

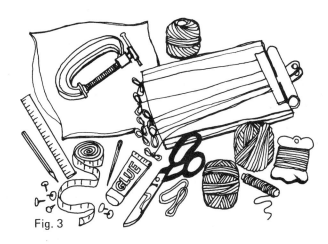
Fig. 3

keeping an even tension. The beauty of a piece of macramé is in the pattern created by the knots – this seems to go without saying. But it means that the texture of the yarn should be secondary to the pattern. Therefore, uneven, nubbly and what are known as 'interest' yarns are not recommended.

It is not necessary to buy 'special' macramé yarns in craft shops; these are often expensive. If you plan to indulge in a fair amount of macramé, it is better to buy yarns in reasonable bulk from marine supply stores, butchers' wholesalers, kitchen or hardware departments, or where-ever they are sold for everyday commercial use. This is the way to keep down the cost of your hobby.

Cotton and linen twines have a long association with the art, and even today, in spite of the introduction of synthetic yarns, are hard to better. Since suitable yarns vary in thickness from the finest cotton or silk thread to rough hemp rope, you must decide on the priorities for the project you have in mind and then choose the appropriate material.

A strong linen cord, for instance, is ideal for the wear and tear that a handbag will have to withstand; a firm cotton twine gives the body and shape necessary for belts to wear with trousers or at hipster level, whereas a supple wool yarn would be suitable for a wallhanging or a shawl.

Before starting work, and especially if you are planning to use a different yarn from the one recommended for a pattern, it is well worth making up a small tension sample. This means that you would mount some threads on a holding cord and follow enough of the pattern – about 3 or 4in square, depending on the scale of the article – to check that the finished item, worked in that yarn and at that tension, would give you the stated measurements.

Obviously, checking tension is less important with a purely decorative item such as a wallhanging but begins to matter more when you are making a garment or fashion accessory. Compare the appearance of your sampler with the photograph of the item, too. Then you can check that you are pulling the knots tight enough, or leaving them loose enough, for the design.

Among the knotting cords to look for are cotton, rayon or nylon seine twine, closely twisted and with very little give, which you can usually obtain from marine supply stores; cotton or wool rug yarn, softer and more supple, from shops supplying weaving materials; linen tufting twine, fine and strong, from upholsterers' suppliers; butchers'

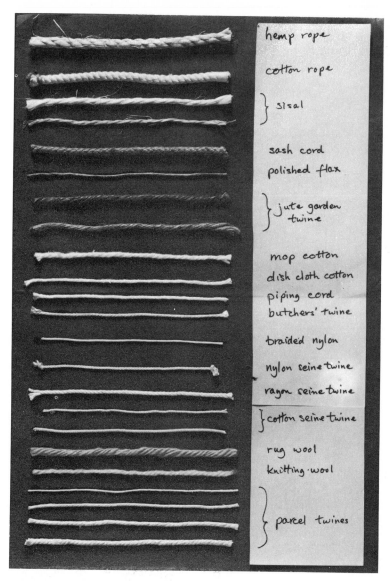

hemp rope

cotton rope

} sisal

sash cord

polished flax

} jute garden twine

mop cotton

dish cloth cotton

piping cord

butchers' twine

braided nylon

nylon seine twine

rayon seine twine

} cotton seine twine

rug wool

knitting wool

} parcel twines

synthetic twine, which is heavy and drapes well, from butchers or their suppliers; cotton or jute parcel twine, from stationers; jute fillis garden twine, slightly shaggy but strong; sisal or hemp rope, piping cord, clothes line, window sash cord, fine garden twine (usually coloured dark green) and cotton, linen or silk crochet thread.

You can also use natural materials such as rushes, dried grasses and raffia, though it is better to save these experiments until you are familiar with the technique and the properties of the other materials. Once you start the work, in fact, you will quickly develop an eye for the possibilities in all kinds of threads and yarns and will constantly be on the look-out for new recruits to your macramé workbox.

Dyeing Yarns

It is very much a matter of personal choice whether you work in natural colours, the unbleached creamy whites of the cotton and linen twines, the slightly more earthy browns of the jute garden twine, or

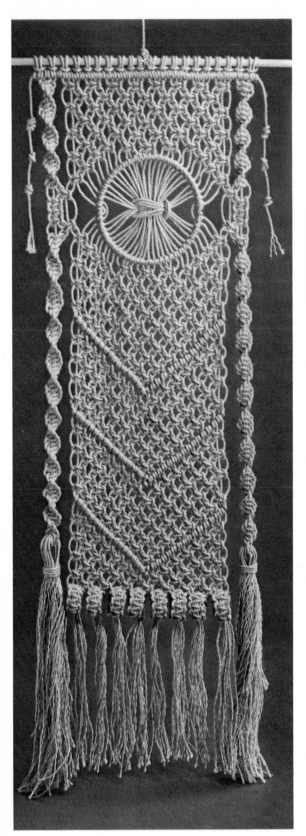

Left: *Rope wallhanging or room divider (see page 53)*
Below: *Grass skirt (see page 63)*

Fig. 4

whether you dye your materials. Certainly some dramatic effects can be achieved by the controlled use of colour, though in this case the knotting pattern variation should be kept to the minimum.

Multi-purpose dyes are most suitable for dyeing yarns, and they are available in a wonderful range of colours, almost fifty shades, in fact. These dyes can be used in hot water, but simmering – for about twenty minutes to half-an-hour – gives greater colour density. Follow the manufacturer's instructions meticulously for the amount of dye to use – it is false economy to buy less than the recommended quantity, because the intensity of the colour will be well below expectations.

Usually, one small tin of dye is needed to $\frac{1}{2}$lb weight of dry material; for an item that required 1lb of yarn, therefore, you would need to allow two tins of dye. Some of the shiny, synthetic yarns will not dye as satisfactorily as the natural fibres and so it is advisable to test a little before committing the whole hank to the dye bath.

One of the most effective, and, incidentally, most economical ways to use dye is to dye material in three stages, as described more fully under the instructions for the handbag. In this way, instead of discarding the dye solution after one use, you use it a second and a third time, simmering more yarn each time in the same solution. The result will be three batches of yarn in strong, medium and pale tones of the same colour.

Since macramé is a traditional craft, it seems more suited to soft, muted colours than to bold statements of vivid contrasts. Look for colours that remind you of a walk across the moors – all the soft blues, purples, pinks and greens – or of a forest when the leaves are falling – consider the ranges of deep greens, golden browns and russets. Slightly muddy colours, like old gold, burnt orange, avocado, crushed strawberry, Air Force blue, all seem to suit the art particularly well.

If tie-dyeing is another of your hobbies, you can happily combine it with macramé by tie-dyeing the yarns you use (Fig. 4). It is possible to control the way the colour falls by cutting the yarn into the lengths you will need and then tying them accordingly. It is probably more fun, though, to dye the yarns in a slightly more random way and let the pattern just happen. Do not try to mix more than two colours – and these should be related in tone – or the effect will be confusing.

When dyeing yarns with a low absorbency, such as some shiny synthetics, or those with a 'coated' finish, it will sometimes be found more satisfactory to dye the finished article rather than the skein of yarn. This is because when yarns do not thoroughly take up the dye, the cut ends tend to reveal the base colour. So it is that a handbag made from yarn dyed dark blue might reveal the off-white or creamy-beige colour of the yarn on the cut ends of the fringing, and look slightly less attractive as a result.

The Basic Knots

Starting work

Measure and cut all yarns first. An easy way to do this is to wrap the yarn round two uprights at a measured distance apart, and then to cut through all the lengths. When you have a large number of cords to cut, this will prove very much quicker than measuring yard by yard with an inch tape.

For long lengths, you can place two dining chairs at the right distance from each other and wind the yarn round the vertical struts; you might find the handles on a cupboard are conveniently spaced, or you can screw two C-clamps on to a kitchen table (Fig. 5).

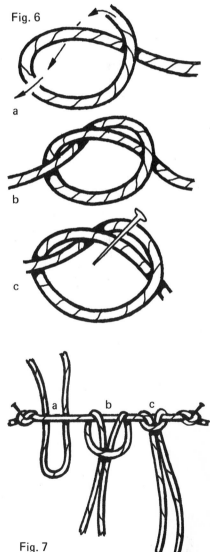

Fig. 6

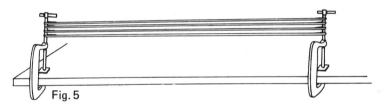

Fig. 5

Select your working surface according to the scale of the item you are to make. Advice is given in the specific pattern instructions. For practice, a piece of soft wall-board, such as a cork tile, about 9in square, is ideal.

Cut a piece of yarn about 12in long, to use as a holding or mounting cord. Make a loop at one end by taking the end over the cord (Fig. 6a), under the cord (Fig. 6b), and through the loop. Push a medium-sized glass-headed pin through the loop and into the top left-hand corner of the working surface and tighten the loop round it (Fig. 6c). This simple loop is known as an Overhand knot, and is extensively used in macramé fringing. Repeat at the other end, pulling the cord taut before tightening the knot round the pin. It is essential that the holding cord is as tight as possible to give a firm edge to the work.

Cut eight lengths of cord each 48in long. This will give you a small practice sample about 6in long. To calculate roughly the length of cord you need for a piece of work, you simply multiply by eight. In the case of our example, the working cords are going to be mounted double on to the holding cord, to give sixteen working lengths of 24in. And then you have to allow three and a half to four times the length of the working cord to be taken up by the knotting.

To mount or set on the threads: take one of the 48in cords, double it and push the loop from top to bottom under the holding cord. Bring the two loose ends down over the holding cord and push them through the loop. Pull them to tighten the loop. Figs. 7a, b and c show this clearly.

Fig. 7

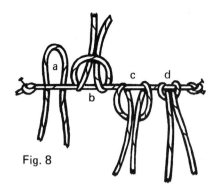

Fig. 8

This knot is known as a Lark's Head knot and is the method most often used for mounting threads. It gives the appearance of a small bead line at the top of the work and can be used to attach threads to a mounting cord of the yarn, to a piece of leather thonging, a dowel or brass rod (for a wallhanging, for example) or to the cross-bar of a buckle.

For a slightly different appearance (the effect of a row of Half-Hitch knots) at the top of the work, you can mount the threads with what is called a Reverse Lark's Head knot. To do this follow Figs. 8a, b, c and d. As you can see the only difference is that you push the doubled thread under the holding cord from the bottom to the top, then take the two loose ends over the holding cord and through the loop; swing the cords down and tighten the knot. It will be seen that in the Lark's Head knot, the two working cords are behind the loop and in the Reverse Lark's Head knot they are in front of it.

Mount all eight threads with a Lark's Head knot, so that you have sixteen working threads. The work will then look like the illustration, Fig. 9.

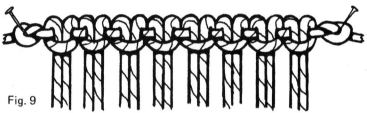

Fig. 9

Flat Knots

We will begin by working Flat knots, using four groups of four working cords to make four strips of Flat knot sennits (a sennit is a term for a form of braid).

Working first with the first four cords on the left-hand side, and imagining that they are numbered 1–4, take the right-hand cord, 4, over cords 2 and 3 (Fig. 10a). Take cord 1 over cord 4, under cords 2 and 3 and out diagonally through the space between cords 3 and 4. Tighten cords 1 and 4 (Fig. 10b). To complete the knot, take the right-hand cord 1, under cords 2 and 3. Take the left-hand cord, 4, under cord 1, over cords 2 and 3 and through the loop between cords 3 and 1 (Fig. 10c). Fig. 10d shows the position of the cords before tightening the knot.

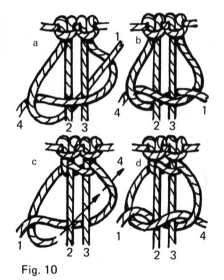

Fig. 10

Take comfort from the fact that no knot is ever as difficult to tie as instructions inevitably make it seem! The knot described above, is in fact a simple reef knot, and is memorised by children by the phrase 'left over right and under; right over left and under'. The only difference here is that the knot is being worked over two 'dormant' cords which do not travel but give substance to the work.

Continue working down the length of cords 1–4 in this way, making a sennit of Flat knots. If your work is interrupted and you forget which way the cords have to travel next, here is an easy way to check. If the last cord on the left of the work comes *under* the loop made on the left, then the next cord on the right has to travel *under* the two dormant or 'filler' cords. If, however, the last cord on the left lies *over* the loop on the left, then the next cord on the right has to travel *over* the filler cords.

For practice, work Flat knots with cords 5–8, 9–12 and 13–16. You will then have a sampler of four rows of Flat knot sennits, which will look like the illustration, Fig. 11.

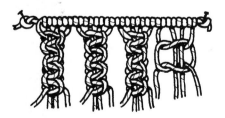

Fig. 11

44

Left: *Draped curtain (see page 55)*
Below: *Olive green and yellow slip mat (see page 19)*

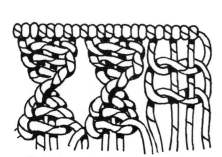

Fig. 12

Half knots

By working the first half of the Flat knot, as described above, repeatedly, and not reversing the cords for the second operation, you can work a row of Half knots. To do this, follow the first part of the instructions for the Flat knot, Figs. 10a and b.

That is to say, take cord 4 over cords 2 and 3; cord 1 over cord 4, under cords 2 and 3, out over cord 4, and tighten the knot. Now, take the right-hand cord over cords 2 and 3, the left-hand cord over it and under cords 2 and 3 and out through the loop (Fig. 12); tighten. A row of these knots will twist and form a spiral – they are a feature of the sailor's belt in Chapter 5. You can see the effect clearly in Fig. 13.

Flat knot patterns

Using exactly the same technique it is possible to make a pattern of Flat knots with the knots running diagonally instead of in a straight line. To do this, work a row of Flat knots using cords 1–4, then 5–8, 9–12 and so on, across the work. Then, leaving aside cords 1 and 2, work a row of Flat knots with cords 3–6, 7–10, 11–14 and so on.

This will give one less knot in the second row, and the two outside cords at each side will be carried down the length of the work in loops. This pattern, known as Alternating Flat knots, and shown clearly in Fig. 14, is the one used in the large hemp and the small woollen wall-hangings in Chapter 3.

A slight variation on the pattern, shown in Fig. 15, is when a double row of Flat knots is worked with each group of 4 cords. To do this, work across the row, tying Flat knots with cords 1–4, 5–8 and so on. Repeat for a second row with the same cords, then leave aside the first two cords and work two rows of Flat knots on cords 3–6, 7–10 and so on.

Simple variations on this technique are endless. If you work several rows of Flat knots on the same groups of cords, then one row on the alternate group, the fabric takes on the appearance of a series of braids drawn together at intervals rather than a continuous close-weave texture.

If you tie a row of Flat knots, then a row of Half knots on the same group of cords, then a Flat knot and a Half knot on the alternate groups, a more open pattern is created, with sharper diagonals. The effect is shown in Fig. 16.

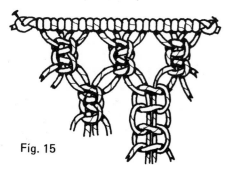

Fig. 13

Fig. 15

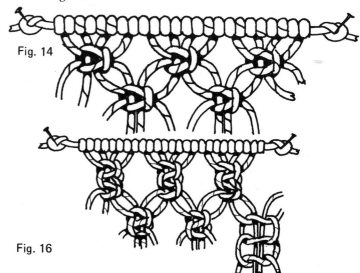

Fig. 14

Fig. 16

The Double Half-Hitch

Just as the Flat knot, or reef knot, has tremendous versatility in macramé, so the Double Half-Hitch can be used in a variety of ways. It is tied over a knot-bearing cord and can be worked horizontally, diagonally or vertically. In various combinations it can be made to form triangles, diamonds, circles and patterns such as leaves or scrolls.

Horizontal Double Half-Hitch

To practise this stitch, mount four cords on a holding cord. A clipboard or piece of cork tile will serve as a working surface. Pin cord 1 across the remaining cords horizontally from left to right, close to the holding cord (Fig. 17a). Take cord 2 over the horizontal cord 1, then behind it, through the loop between cords 1 and 2 (Fig. 17b). This completes one Half-Hitch. Take cord 2 over cord 1 again, to the right of the first knot, under the cord and out through the loop (Fig. 17c). Tighten the knot (Fig. 17d). This completes a Double Half-Hitch.

Leave cord 2 and proceed with cord 3, making a Double Half-Hitch knot in exactly the same way, over the horizontal cord 1. Continue along the row, working with each cord in succession, and always over the knot-bearing cord, 1.

To work a row of Horizontal Double Half-Hitch from right to left, the process is exactly the same but in reverse. That is to say that the last cord on the right-hand side, cord 8 in this case, is pinned horizontally across the work; Double Half-Hitches are worked across it (Fig. 18) with cords 7, 6 and so on, until cord 1 has been worked.

To work a second row of Horizontal Double Half-Hitch knots under the first, you simply turn the knot-bearing cord and pin it parallel with the first row, then proceed knotting across it as before (Figs. 19a and b).

Once you have learned this technique, and practised pulling the knots evenly so that your rows of cording are firm and straight, it is a simple matter to work Diagonal Half-Hitches. This just means that the knot-bearing cord is pinned diagonally instead of straight across the work and the line of cording is worked over it.

To practise this knot, mount four cords on to a holding cord, giving you eight working ends. Pin cord 1 across the others at an angle of 45deg and work a Double Half-Hitch over it with each cord in turn, starting with cord 2 and working through to cord 8 (Figs. 20a and b). To work a second parallel row, pin cord 2 below the row of cording you have just worked and work over it with cords 3–8 in that order (Figs. 20c and d). The knot bearers usually become knotting (tying) cords in succeeding rows to keep rows from becoming shorter.

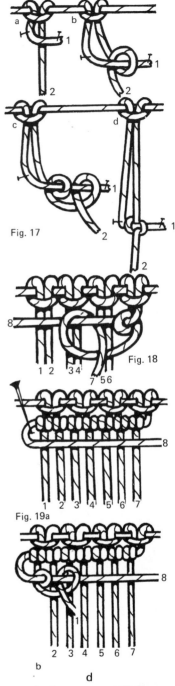

Fig. 17

Fig. 18

Fig. 19a

b

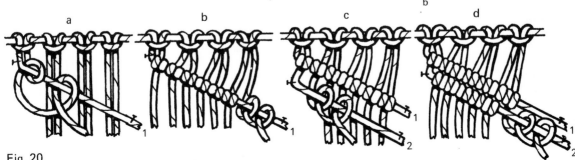

a   b   c   d

Fig. 20

Corded stool (see page 56)

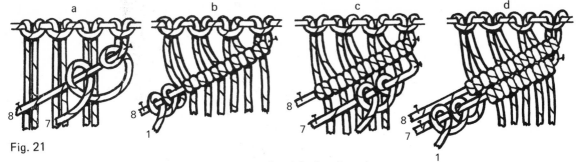

Fig. 21

To work the diagonal in the other direction, pin the right-hand cord, in this case cord 8, diagonally across the work and then work Double Half-Hitches over it with cords 7–1 in that order (Figs. 21a and b). For a second row, pin cord 7 parallel with the row of knotting and work over it with cords 6–1 (Figs. 21c and d).

Once you have mastered the art of working Double Half-Hitches, you will be able to follow patterns in which these rows of 'cording' cross. They give a most effective fabric for belts, for example.

To work a sample of crossing diagonals, mount 8 cords on to a holding cord, giving you 16 working cords. Divide the cords into two groups of 8. Start by using cord 1, the left-hand cord, as the knot bearer. Hold it diagonally over cords 2–8, at an angle of 45deg, making sure to keep it taut. Tie Double Half-Hitches over it with cords 2–8 in that order.

Now cord 16 becomes the knot bearer. Hold it taut across the work, over cords 15–9. Work Double Half-Hitches over it with cords 15–9 (Fig. 22).

It is important to make a neat and secure join where the cords cross. Cords 1 and 16 must be neatly knotted together. Place cord 16 over cord 1 and hold it taut with the left hand. Tie a Double Half-Hitch over it with cord 1 (Fig. 23). By now you have completed a V-shaped section of cording.

To continue the X formation, cord 16 again becomes the knot bearer. Tie Double Half-Hitches over it with cords 8–2, in that order, holding or pinning the knot bearer taut across the work, in line with the row of cording already worked. Now, to complete the X, cord 1 becomes the knot bearer and cords 9–15 are tied over it. Fig. 24 shows the completed pattern, with a row of horizontal cording beneath the cross.

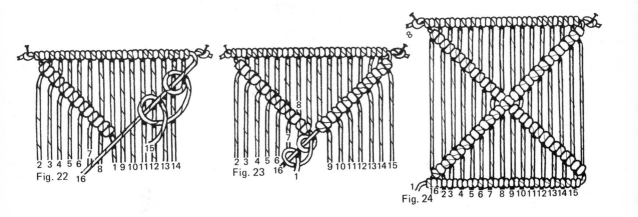

Fig. 22 Fig. 23 Fig. 24

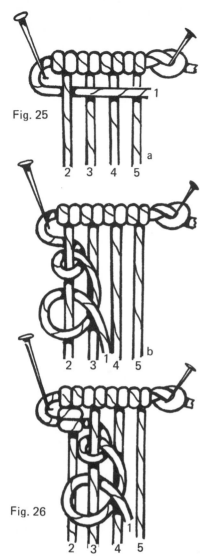

Fig. 25

Fig. 26

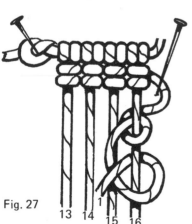

Fig. 27

Vertical Double Half-Hitch

As can be seen from the illustrations, the knots in Horizontal Double Half-Hitch go from top to bottom across a horizontal knot bearer. In Vertical Double Half-Hitches, the knots go in a side-to-side direction across vertical knot bearers. Whereas the knot-bearer remains constant in both Horizontal and Diagonal working, and the remaining cords are knotted over it, in vertical working, one cord (either the left- or right-hand one) is the knotting or travelling cord and each of the others in turn becomes a knot bearer.

Allowance has to be made for this fact in calculating the length of the knotting cord before cutting – roughly half as long again as the other cords.

To make a practice sampler, again attach a holding cord to a working surface and mount four cords on it, to give eight working ends. Push a pin into the working surface, between cords 1 and 2, just below the Lark's Head knots. Take cord 1 round the pin (Fig. 25a) and *under* cord 2. Hold cord 2, which is now the knot bearer, taut, and make a Double Half-Hitch over it with cord 1.

This means that cord 1 travels under cord 2, over it, under and through the loop; over cord 2 again, under it and out through the loop (Fig. 25b). Still keeping the knot-bearing cord taut, tighten the knot firmly. It is important to retain an even tension in knotting.

Continuing to knot with cord 1, take this cord under cord 3 and work a Double Half-Hitch as described, keeping cord 3 taut as you do so (Fig. 26). Tighten the knot.

When you have completed a row of Vertical Double Half-Hitches, and if you wish to work another, remove the pin from the left-hand side of the work and push it between cords 8 and 7 (or the last two right-hand cords, depending on the number of threads mounted). Cord 8 becomes the travelling or knotting cord, cord 7 the first knot-bearer (Fig. 27) and the process is repeated back across the row.

Around the Home

You have now learned the two basic knots used in macramé, and enough variations of their use to make any number of decorative and attractive items for yourself or the home. Probably one of the easiest ways to gain confidence and a feeling of instant achievement is to make something that uses sennits, or braids, for once started on a row of these, the work progresses fairly rapidly and is practically fault-proof.

Our suggestion is for a beaded door or window curtain which can be readily adapted to any size you wish to make it. When calculating the width, estimate that each of the sennits is about 1in wide. Allowance has to be made for this fact in calculating the length of the knotting cord before cutting – roughly twice as long as the other cords.

The curtain uses Lark's Head knots – the cords are mounted on to a bamboo cane – Horizontal Double Half-Hitch, Flat knots, Half knots and Overhand knots, all very familiar territory by now.

When working with long cords for a full-length door curtain, it will be necessary to bundle these up to a manageable working length. The usual way of doing this, so that the twine is safe from tangling, is to wrap the cords in what is called a bobbin. If you wrap the cord from the middle to the end and fasten it with a rubber band, you can feed out the cord as you need it without unravelling the whole bundle.

Wind the cord, 'butterfly' fashion, into a figure eight around your thumb and fourth finger or, when very long lengths or heavy twine are being used, from the thumb around the elbow. Fasten securely in the middle with a tightly twisted rubber band (Figs. 28a and b).

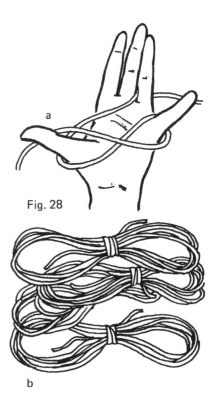

Fig. 28

a

b

Door Curtain

Measurements
The curtain as shown is 29in wide and 74in long.

Materials
4lb ball of 4-ply natural-coloured jute. If you cannot buy twine by the pound, the curtain requires about 810yd. This length would vary, of course, with the weight and thickness of the string, if you chose a different quality; 7 hollow bamboo canes, about 4ft long, with a diameter of about $\frac{3}{4}$ to $\frac{5}{8}$in. Buy these from a garden supply stores; a few natural-coloured wooden beads, $\frac{3}{8}$in in diameter (optional); woodworking vice (if available); fret (coping) saw; fine sandpaper; elastic bands.

Method

Choose the sturdiest of the canes to mount the curtain and saw the others in random lengths of between 1 and 3in, to use as beads. The easiest way to saw the canes is to hold each one in a small woodworking vice, using the edge of the tool as a guide for the saw blade. A fret (coping) saw does the job well.

You will find that at the 'joints' the bamboo is solid right through; these small sections must be discarded because the beads must be hollow for threading: the hole has to be wide enough to take two thicknesses of the string. Smooth the edges of the bamboo beads by rubbing with a piece of fine sandpaper.

Cut fifty-four lengths of twine, each 15yd long. Do not double the cords in half as you have in practice samplers. To give the length needed for the first and fourth cords in each group, fold the cords one-fifth of the way along the length, so that each pair is 12yd long on the outside and 3yd long on the inside. In each group, therefore, the length will be as follows: cord 1, 12yd; cord 2, 3yd; cord 3, 3yd and cord 4, 12yd. Mount the cords on the reserved garden cane in groups of two – to give four working cords – with a Lark's Head knot.

Bundle the longest (12yd) lengths into bobbins as described, and fasten with elastic bands. Leave a working length of about 24in.

Suspend the bamboo pole from a picture rail, across a doorway or on cup hooks. Cut an extra 44in length of twine, secure it with pins just under the cane, and work a row of Horizontal Double Half-Hitch knots over it with all fifty-four knotting cords. String a bamboo bead on each of the overhanging ends of this horizontal knot-bearing cord, secure with a knot and trim ends.

To make the first sennit

Work with the first four cords on the left-hand side, cords 1 to 4. Slip four bamboo beads on to cords 2 and 3 so that they can be drawn up as needed. The aim of a design of this kind is to plan a random look! As you work across the curtain, check that the beads are not, by accident, falling all in a straight line. Devise a means of holding the two knot-bearing cords taut – by standing on them or tying them round your waist. It is important that they are held under slight tension.

Work about twelve to fourteen Flat knots first, then draw up a bamboo bead. Secure the bead with a Half knot. Two cords will be threaded through the bead and the other two will travel outside it.

Continue tying Half knots, with the left-hand cord always on top of the knot bearers. This will make the sennit twist in a spiral.

Push up a bead at intervals and occasionally thread in small wooden beads if used; continue working the spiral twist until the sennit measures 72in long – or the length desired. Finish the sennit with an Overhand knot tied with all four cords.

Using the cords in groups of four, continue making sennits in this way, varying the number of Flat knots at the top of each braid and the distance between the beads. To vary still further, work short lengths of Flat knots instead of Half knot spirals between some of the beads.

Trim all ends so that the lower edge of the curtain is completely level. Cut mounting cane to the correct length and hang on hooks in the doorway or at the window.

Note that, if a dowel is used instead of a bamboo cane for mounting the threads, it should be slightly thicker; a hollow cane is less likely than a solid rod to sag with the weight of the twine.

Rope Wallhanging or Room Divider

Anyone who would describe herself as all fingers and thumbs, and perhaps be diffident about starting a piece of delicate work, must surely feel at home with this larger-than-life-sized wallhanging. It is made from ⅞in hemp rope and positively grows before your eyes.

Measurements
The hanging measures 30in wide and 7ft long.

Materials
240yd ⅞in (circumference) hemp rope; 1 broom handle or 1in dowel, 36in long; 1 lampshade ring or any stiff wire – 13in in diameter; strong leather gardening gloves (these are essential for working with an abrasive material such as this tough rope); large pins; string.

Method
Cut 20 cords, each 15yd long. This is a generous allowance, but it will be seen that the cords are quickly used up in the work. The ends will be used for the side tassels.

Mount the cords on the broom handle or dowel with Lark's Head knots in the middle of each cord. This will give you 40 working cords.

If possible, suspend the work from hooks in a doorway, arch or other open space. There is no question of working a piece this size on a working surface, and it is not very easy to work against a wall. Bundle each cord up and tie into a bobbin with string.

Cut a 54in length of the rope and lay it over the mounted cords. Pin it at the left-hand side, or wind it round the dowel, to secure.

Work a row of Horizontal Double Half-Hitch cording over the knot bearer, just below the dowel. With the four left-hand cords, work a spiral sennit of twenty-three Half knots. Allow the work to twist as it proceeds. With the four right-hand cords, work a matching spiral sennit of twenty-three Half knots.

1st–6th rows: With the remaining 32 cords, work Alternating Flat knot pattern. The 1st, 3rd and 5th rows have 8 knots, the 2nd, 4th and 6th rows have 7 knots.

7th row: Work 2 Flat knots with 8 left-hand cords and 2 Flat knots with 8 right-hand cords.

8th row: Leave aside first 2 cords, work 1 Flat knot with cords 3, 4, 5 and 6; leave aside cords 7–26; work Flat knots with cords 27, 28, 29 and 30. Leave aside last 2 cords.

9th row: Work 1 Flat knot with cords 1–4. Leave aside the intervening cords and work 1 Flat knot with cords 29–32.

10th row: Check that the 2 Half knot spirals are the same length as the Flat knot panel. If they are not, work more Half-knots on the spiral if necessary, to adjust. Leaving aside the first 2 cords of spiral, work 1 Flat knot with cords 3 and 4 of the spiral and the first 2 cords of the panel.

Repeat on the right-hand side of the hanging, tying 1 Flat knot with the last 2 cords of the panel and cords 1 and 2 of the spiral.

Work 3 Flat knots with all 4 cords of each of the spirals. Work 1 Flat knot with the last 2 cords of the spiral and the first 2 cords of the panel on the left-hand side. Repeat on the right-hand side with the last 2 cords of the panel and the first 2 of the spiral. Leave aside the 4 cords

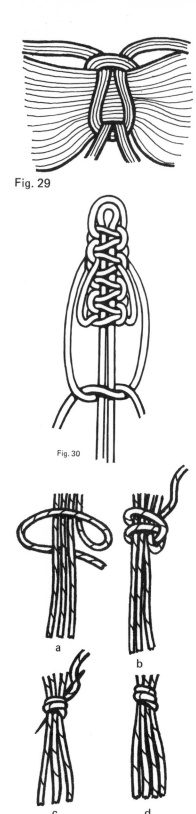

Fig. 29

Fig. 30

Fig. 31

from the panel and the outer 2 cords of the panel on both sides of the work.

To work the top half of the ring, pin the lampshade ring or wire circle over the 28 working cords remaining in the panel.

Using the ring as the knot bearer, work Horizontal Double Half-Hitches over it with all cords. This will fill the top half of the ring.

Gather the centre 18 cords together and tie a large Flat knot over them with 3 cords from either side (see Fig. 29). This leaves 2 cords on either side that are not included in the pattern.

Continue by working Horizontal Double Half-Hitches over the bottom half of the ring with all 29 cords, spreading them evenly out from the gathering knot.

Take 2 cords back from the 6 you have left aside. You will now have 32 working cords in the panel again. Tie 1 Flat knot on either side of the ring with the outside 4 cords on each side.

Next row: Leave aside the first 2 cords on either side and tie 1 Flat knot next to the ring with the next 4 cords.

Next row: Tie 2 Flat knots on either side of the ring.

Next row: Leave aside the first 2 cords and tie 7 Flat knots; leave aside the last 2 cords.

Next row: Tie 8 Flat knots across the work.

Next row: Leave aside first and last 2 cords and tie 7 Flat knots. Repeat last 2 rows once more.

Next row: Keeping in the Alternating Flat knot pattern, tie 5 Flat knots in the centre of the work.

Next row: Tie 4 Flat knots in the centre panel.

Next row: Tie 3 Flat knots in the centre.

Next row: Tie 2 Flat knots in the centre.

Next row: Bring the centre panel to a point with 1 Flat knot.

To work the cording, take the left-hand cord from the point where you started to decrease the Alternating Flat knot pattern, and lay it along the left-hand edge of the panel, diagonally across the work. Work Horizontal Double Half-Hitch over it with all the cords, down to the middle of the work.

Taking the cord on the right-hand side, lay this along the opposite side of the panel and work Horizontal Double Half-Hitch over it.

Continue the Alternating Flat knot pattern on either side of the cording. Below the point of cording, you will have 8 knots in the row.

Beginning with the next row, start decreasing again until this panel, too, comes to a point with 1 Flat knot in the centre.

Repeat the Horizontal Double Half-Hitch cording with first the left-hand cord as knot bearer, then the right-hand one.

Work a further panel of Alternating Flat knots, again beginning to decrease as soon as you have reached an 8-knot row.

Repeat the V-shaped pattern of Horizontal Double Half-Hitches. Continue in the Alternating Flat knot pattern until you reach the 8-knot row. Work 1 alternating row of 7 Flat knots.

To finish panel:

With 4 left-hand cords, work a sennit of 8 Flat knots. Roll up the sennit and push 2 centre cords through the top knot of the sennit. Pull it up tightly to form a ring (Fig. 30).

Make a tassel by coil-wrapping 3 cords with the other one (Fig. 31a and b) and pull through (Fig. 31c and d).

Repeat this section across the work, with remaining 7 groups of cords.

You will now have 8 coils of Flat knots and 8 coil-wrapped tassels. Trim the ends of the rope to between 12 and 16in and fray out the ends. Return to the spiral sennits to finish.

Continue the sennits in spiral pattern down to the last row of cording. Measure to check when this point has been reached. The tying cords will probably now be rather short.

Cut 24 lengths of rope each 2yd long. Divide into 2 for each tassel. Take the 4 cords of the left-hand sennit and divide in 2; tie 1 loose knot (a Half-knot without a core).

Lay ends over the knot and tighten. Draw the lengths of cord together for the tassel. Arrange as neatly as possible and make a short coil wrap with one of the cords. Pull this as tightly as you can, as this holds the tassel in place. Trim to the length of the panel and fray the ends to make the tassel splay out.

Repeat with the remaining 12 cords for the second tassel. Finish the ends of the loose cord at the top with a small Overhand or coil knot.

Repeated in Wool

It is difficult to believe that the duplicate wallhanging worked in rug wool follows exactly the same instruction as those for the giant-sized hanging. This is a good example of the adaptability of macramé: the scale and texture of the yarn, not the technique or pattern, are the deciding factors in the scale of the finished article. Because of the basic simplicity of the Alternating Flat knot pattern, this hanging could equally well be worked in wool dyed in several shades, or tie-dyed. The wool shown in the photograph was, in fact, bleached to a pale grey-blue.

Measurements
The wallhanging is 9in wide by 28in long, including the fringe.

Materials
Approximately $\frac{1}{2}$lb rug wool; 15in long dowel; a small lampshade ring, $5\frac{1}{2}$in in diameter, or strong wire to make a ring.

Method
Cut 20 lengths of rug wool each 5yd long. Double the cords and mount them on to the dowel with Lark's Head knots.

Follow the instructions for the wallhanging in hemp rope. Cut a 26in long piece of the wool and thread it through the cording at the back of the hanging. Knot the wool in the centre and hang by this thread.

Draped Curtain

This curtain, made for the small window of a bathroom in a modern house, shows a quite different effect of the art of macramé. It has the transparency and softness of a fine draped fabric, combined with the strength and durability of a synthetic yarn. If the sizes of the windows in your house are too daunting for a piece of work of this kind, it is surely decorative enough to be used as a wallhanging. It would look stunning against a plain dark background.

Measurements

The curtain is 23in sq when draped. Spread flat, before draping, it measures 20 by 30in.

Materials

A 13oz ball of butcher's twine or any similar synthetic string; an old brass stair-rod, length of brass tube, bamboo or curtain rod, 24in long; a large piece (roughly 24 by 36in) of soft wallboard or corrugated cardboard for the working surface; pins; ruler; pencil or felt-tip pen; heavy tapestry or wool needle; clear adhesive.

Method

It is essential to choose a twine with a heavy weight ratio to achieve the swagged effect of the drape; cut 56 2yd lengths of the twine. The curtain is worked from side to side. Double the cords and mount them by pinning each one in the middle on to the right-hand side of the working surface. This will give you 112 working cords.

This project is not mounted on to a holding cord.

Cut 3 separate knotting cords of about 10yd each – the length may vary slightly: the aim is to add new knotting cord invisibly inside the corded rows. Pin one 10yd cord at the right-side of the cords and work a row of Vertical Half-Hitch knots from right to left.

Work a row of Vertical Half-Hitch from left to right. Just below this, work a row of Horizontal Double Half-Hitch from right to left.

Now pin these 3 closely-worked rows securely to the board and measure 9in along the vertical strings. Draw a guide line on the board with a pencil or felt-tip pen. Your knotting cord is at the left-hand side. Bring it down alongside the other strings and at the line start knotting a row of Vertical Half-Hitch from left to right.

Next row: Work a row of Horizontal Double Half-Hitch from right to left, adding a new knotting cord. To do this, lay it alongside the short length of cord, knot over both for a few knots, by which time the new cord can take over. Trim off the end of the used cord.

Next row: Work a row of Vertical Half-Hitch from left to right.

Measure a further 9in along the board, draw a guide line and repeat the 3 cording rows close together. Measure another 9in along the board and draw a guide line. Bring the knotting cord down the side and work a row of Horizontal Double Half-Hitch, adding a new leader if required. Work 2 rows of Vertical Half-Hitch.

There will now be 112 cords to thread into the back of the work. Use a heavy tapestry or wool needle. Cut off ends and touch with a dab of clear adhesive.

Take some of the short ends to make double hanging loops at the left end of each triple row of cording, making sure that they are just big enough for the curtain rod you are using. Thread ends securely through back of knots and touch ends with glue. Alternatively, you can sew on small brass curtain rings and slide these over the rod.

Corded Stool

Macramé is an ideal medium for re-seating stools and chairs; heavy quality parcel twine makes a fabric which is both attractive and durable and these instructions can be adapted to suit any chair seat or back.

Measurements
The stool top measures 12in sq.

Materials
For this size of stool, you need about 100yd of heavy parcel string, 3/16in in diameter; crochet hook; knitting needle; boot lacer (optional); clear adhesive.

Method
Cut 14 cords each 5yd long and one – part of which will be the long knot-bearing cord – 20yd long. Mount the 14 cords on one side of the stool with Lark's Head knots.

Mount the long cord at the left end of the others so that one end of it is the same length – $2\frac{1}{2}$yd – as the others, and the other longer end is on the left. You now have 1 knot-bearing cord and 29 knotting cords.

Lay the long left-hand cord over the others and begin tying Horizontal Double Half-Hitches across the row. When you reach the side rail, tie a Lark's Head knot over it with the knot-bearing cord; work Horizontal Double Half-Hitches back from right to left. Tie Lark's Head knot over left-hand rail.

Continue in this way along the length of the stool, pulling the knot-bearing cord as taut as possible over side rails.

When you have corded all the way across the stool – in this case 24 rows – tie Lark's Head knots over the rail with each knotting cord. These will be very close together, and a crochet hook is useful to bring cord from top to underside.

Turn stool upside-down and, using the same knot-bearing cord, tie a row of Horizontal cording along the underside to secure knotting cords. Thread ends under one previous row of knots on underside and clip ends, touching with glue. A knitting needle is useful here to loosen knots.

Now you must fill in the spaces between the Lark's Head knots on the other three sides of the stool. Cut a piece of string about 15yd long (going round each spindle rail twice, for each knot uses a lot of string) and tie Lark's Head knots all round the other 3 sides in between the original knots. Thread all ends in underneath and touch with glue. A football lacer is a great help with this final threading.

Sisal Rug

Here are instructions for making a strong, durable rug in sisal twine. The fabric, created in an Alternating Flat knot pattern, is tough enough for heavy-duty areas, such as kitchen, bathroom or passage. If preferred, the yarn can be dyed before use, but we show the rug in natural twine.

Measurements
The rug is 21in wide, and 68in long, including the 7in fringe.

Materials
A 6lb ball of 3-ply sisal twine; drawing board, for working surface; adhesive tape; elastic bands.

Method

Cut 80 cords, each 8yd long. Mount the cords singly and at the middle of the working surface. A simple way to do this is to tape them to a drawing board or surface of similar size. Bundle the ends into bobbins, leaving 24in working lengths. When a few rows have been knotted the tape is removed and the rug moved up the board. It can then be held in place with heavy books or scale weights; the weight of the string itself also helps to keep the work in place.

1st and 2nd row: Work 20 Flat knots, across all the cords.

3rd and 4th rows: Leave aside the first 2 cords and tie 19 Flat knots across the work. Leave aside the last 2 cords.

5th and 6th rows: Repeat 1st and 2nd rows.

7th row: Using left-hand cord as knot bearer, work a row of Horizontal Double Half-Hitch knots across. After this, the knot bearer reverts to a knotting cord again.

8th and 9th rows: Work 20 Flat knots across the row.

10th and 11th rows: Work 19 Flat knots.

Repeat 8th and 9th rows; 10th and 11th rows, then 8th and 9th rows once more. This completes the centre section of the rug, with a pattern of Alternating Flat knots.

Next row: Using the right-hand cord as knot bearer, work a row of Horizontal Double Half-Hitch. This cord will now be getting short. This is the best place to add another. Cut a 5yd length and lay it next to the knot bearer. Knot over the 2 cords until the end of the row. At that point, the new length becomes the knotting cord and the short end is trimmed off.

Continue by working 7 *double* rows of Alternating Flat knots (that is, 14 rows), beginning and ending with 20-knot rows.

Next row: Using the left-hand cord as knot bearer, work a row of Horizontal Double Half-Hitch.

Continue by working 9 double rows (18 rows) of Alternating Flat knots, beginning and ending with 20-knot rows.

Next row: Using the right-hand cord as knot bearer, work a row of Horizontal Double Half-Hitch across. Work 1 more double row (that is to say, 2 rows) of 20 Flat knots.

Next row: Using the left-hand cord as knot bearer, work a row of Horizontal Double Half-Hitch.

Next row: Using the right-hand cord as knot bearer, work a row of Horizontal Double Half-Hitch.

Last row: Using the left-hand cord as knot bearer, work a row of Horizontal Double Half-Hitch.

To make the fringe

Lay the first 2 cords to the right, the second 2 cords to the left and so on, all the way across, laying the first group over the second and under the third and so on. Tie an Overhand knot with the second and fourth groups, about $1\frac{1}{2}$in from the last row of cording.

Tie an Overhand knot with the first and fifth groups, the third and eighth groups, and so on across. Trim the fringe to 8in from the Overhand knots and fray out.

To complete the other half of the rug, turn the work on the working board. Using the right-hand cord as knot bearer, work a row of Horizontal Double Half-Hitch across.

Now that you have reversed the work, you will have to reverse the direction in which you tie the Flat knots, otherwise you will find that

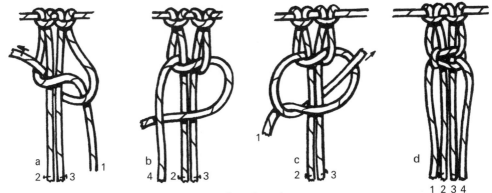

Fig. 33

a

2 3 1

b

4 2 3

c

2 3 1

d

1 2 3 4

in one half of the rug you have right-hand Flat knots and in the other left-hand Flat knots.

To work the knot in the opposite way, take the left-hand cord, 1, over cords 2 and 3. Take cord 4 over cord 1, under cords 2 and 3 and out diagonally through the space between cords 1 and 2. Tighten cords 1 and 4. To complete the knot, take the left-hand cord, 4, under cords 2 and 3. Take the right-hand cord, 1, under cord 4, over cords 2 and 3 and through the loop between cords 2 and 4 (Fig. 33a, b, c and d).

Work a section of 5 *double* rows of Alternating Flat knots (that is, 10 rows), then a row of Horizontal Double Half-Hitch cording.

Work 7 double rows of Alternating Flat knots (14 rows), a further row of Horizontal cording (it will probably be necessary to add a new knot bearer at this stage), then a section of 9 double rows of Alternating Flat knots (18 rows) and a further row of Horizontal Double Half-Hitch. Finally, work one double row of Flat knots (2 rows).

To finish the rug, work 3 rows of Horizontal Double Half-Hitches, and complete the fringe as described for the other end.

Jewellery

We have seen that macramé knotting and fringing can be put to many sensible, hard-wearing and practical uses for the home, but equally it can be worked to make decorative articles purely for adornment. Few things could be more bright and frivolous than the necklace and bracelet set, shown on page 29 with multi-coloured beads set in coloured parcel twine. Other knots and techniques adapt well to jewellery. Sennits or braids can be used to make necklaces, chain belts and bracelets, and beads or motif samples – even a first attempt at a knotting pattern – can be hung as fobs or pendants.

Measurements
The necklace band measures 14in, plus $4\frac{1}{2}$in ties. The bracelet measures $8\frac{1}{2}$in, plus tassel.

Materials
2 small balls of coloured parcel twine – about 50yd; about 120 wooden beads in assorted colours and sizes; working base – (a piece of soft wallboard, or old cushion).

Method
For the necklace:
Cut 2 holding cords, each 1yd long. Mount them together on the working base. Cut 44 working cords, each 2ft long and mount them on the double holding cord with Lark's Head knots. Cut 1 working cord 42in long. Working out from the centre of the neckband, mount this cord just below the Lark's Head knots and work a row of Horizontal cording. Let this cording gently curve the necklace into a circular shape. The ends of this long working cord now become knotting cords at each end, so you have 112 knotting cords. Work a row of 28 Flat knots across.

String 1 medium-size bead on the 2 centre cords of each knot, or on only 1 cord, if the hole in the bead is not large enough. Tie a Flat knot beneath each bead to secure it.

Working from the left, and leaving aside the first 2 cords, work another row of Flat knots across, using 2 cords from each adjoining knot in the previous row. This makes the Alternating Flat knot pattern.

Tie a Flat knot with the 2 left-hand cords (the knot will not be tied over knot-bearing cords, as usual), thread a medium-size bead and secure it with a Flat knot. String a smaller bead on each of the 2 cords, secure with Overhand knots as close as possible to each bead. Clip ends. This completes the left-hand side of the necklace.

String a large bead on to each 2 centre-cords of the 27 groups of 4 cords and tie a Flat knot below each one to secure. With the 2 cords on the right-hand side, tie a plain Flat knot, thread on a medium-size bead and secure with a Flat knot. Thread a smaller bead on each of the 2 cords and secure with Overhand knots. Trim the ends.

String a small bead on to each of the cords, pushing them as close as possible to the large beads. Secure each one with 2 Overhand knots. Trim ends. With the ends of holding cords, tie Half-Hitch chains to the end, string on a medium-size bead and secure with Overhand knots.

For the bracelet:
Cut 2 centre cords each 1yd long. Cut a tying cord 3yd long. String a large bead on to the 2 centre cords and double them. The bead will fasten the bangle. Now you will tie over 4 cords.

Fold the tying cord in half and start tying Flat knots over the centre cord. You will have 2 tying cords of $1\frac{1}{2}$yd each.

String beads in assorted sizes at random on to the tying cord so that they lie on either side and sometimes on top of the bracelet.

When the bracelet measures $7\frac{1}{2}$in, divide the strings in half and with each set of 3 cords tie 5 Half-Hitches. This means tying 1 string with 2 in each set. Bring all together and tie 2 Flat knots. You have now made the buttonhole to fasten with the bead.

Finish with an Overhand knot. String a bead on each of the 6 cords and secure with 2 Overhand knots about $1\frac{1}{2}$in below the buttonhole.

Always in Fashion

It is in the world of fashion that macramé has enjoyed such an exciting revival. And this is appropriate, since some of the earliest-known examples of the art are fringes to wearing apparel. In the British Museum, for example, there is an Assyrian frieze dated about 850 BC which shows elaborate knotting around the bottom of a warrior's tunic. This technique was used in the Middle East as a way of finishing the unwoven ends of fabric to give a decorative, lacy border instead of simply a hem.

It's a fashion that has caught on throughout the ages, for each time macramé has found new favour, intricate fringes have been one of the main features of the craze. In Victorian times, for instance, they were applied to table-cloths, chair backs, mantel covers and, of course, those nostalgic 'granny' shawls.

The garment we have chosen to begin this chapter is, admittedly, a far cry from any Victorian heirloom. It is not quite a skirt, not quite a shawl, and not nearly a necklace. Yet it can be worn, over a dark-coloured trouser suit or leotard, in any of those ways. Perhaps it is best described as 'body jewellery', and versatile at that.

It is made from a heavy synthetic twine, the kind that butchers use. For them, the main advantage of the yarn is the fact that it is moisture-resistant; we chose it because it is heavier than natural yarns; the weight makes the garment drape and swing and swish most effectively. This is one of the few exceptions we have found to the rule that, by and large, natural fibres work better than synthetic yarns in macramé.

This must surely be one of the most 'instant effect' garments ever. It is simple and quick enough to make for a teenage party or to adapt for a children's fancy dress party: it's a natural as a hula-hula-girl skirt. There is only a simple cording along the top, five diamond-shaped panels of Flat knots, and the rest is left to the drape of the twine and the way you wear it.

A similar Flat knot fabric is used to make what we describe as a 'sailor's belt' – because it is a copy of one that Anna North's uncle made over fifty years ago. The spiral twist panels – there are three – break up the texture and give an extra dimension to the design, probably worked out on a lonely watch at sea all those years ago.

One intensely practical advantage of the design is that the loop at one end makes it possible to change the buckle. So you can make the belt, as we have done, in a neutral colour and match any number of coloured wooden or plastic buckles to different outfits. The loop is slipped over the bar and prong and the length of the belt pulled through.

The other belt – also with a seafaring look – is made of a pattern of Josephine knots which gives a flat, firm fabric. It does tend to stretch (and of course become narrower) under pressure so should not be nipped in too tightly, Victorian style, at the waist.

Buckle or sash belts are the easiest items to design for yourself since they are, in effect, simply braids. Therefore, if you see a braid pattern you like as part of a wallhanging, curtain or even floor rug, you can readily adapt it to make a belt length. With experience, of course, you can vary the width and texture considerably by choosing yarns of quite different weight. The enormous variety in the relative sizes of the two wallhangings in Chapter 7, made in exactly the same pattern but with different yarns, illustrates this point.

There is no end to the variety of handbag types and styles that can be made in macramé – the knotting makes a firm, strong fabric that wears well and teams perfectly with today's feeling for casual clothes – trouser-suits and jeans.

The bag photographed here was inspired by a Mexican design made up in stripes of traditionally bright yet toning colours – red, yellow, purple, white and orange.

Feeling that this was, perhaps, going a little too far, we planned ours in muted, natural shades which Anna North dyed, not quite at random. She started with three basic colours of multi-purpose dye, dark green, brown and golden brown, and dyed lengths in three stages of the dye. That is, some first in the dye at full-strength, more later, when the dye effect was less intense, and more later still when the colour is much diluted. This way, the colours are perfectly related to each other – and you don't have to buy too many tins of dye for the one item. The instructions for the skirt, the belts and the bag follow.

Grass Skirt

This is a wear-as-you-please garment, but we designed it to be a zingy skirt to wear over a leotard or trousers. As we later discovered, it looks equally effective draped round the shoulders with the tie at the front, shawl or cape style, or the other way round, like a huge Cleopatra necklace, with the tie at the back.

Measurements
The skirt is made to fit a 26in waist. And perhaps this is the point where restraint should enter in: it really does look more effective on the beanpoles! As shown, the skirt measures 39in in length from waist cord. This is ankle length on average heights. The cords could, of course, be shortened to make a knee- or midi-length garment.

Materials
1 13oz ball of butcher's twine (a synthetic yarn) or any string heavy enough to drape well; working surface, a piece of soft wallboard, corrugated cardboard or thick sheet foam – the surface needs to be long and narrow, about 27in by 5 or 6in; clear adhesive; pins.

Friendly neighbourhood butchers will probably sell you a ball of the twine, but don't ask for it in supermarkets or your local chain store. To test other yarns for drape, unroll a little, hold it in a loop and look closely to see how it behaves. If it hangs limply, with some creases, it will not give the best effect. What you want is a twine that hangs with obvious, positive weight.

Method

Cut 2 holding cords, each 2yd 9in long and 78 cords, each 2yd 24in long. Double the holding cord. Working from the middle of the holding cord, mount the cords double with Lark's Head knots. You will now have 156 working cords.

Pin the holding cord to your working surface at both ends. Cut a separate knot leader 36in long and lay it over the knotting cords, pinning it to secure at the left-hand side.

Work a row of Horizontal Double Half-Hitch cording as close as possible to the Lark's Head knots. Work 2 rows of Flat knots in Alternating Flat knot pattern.

To work the 2 triangular panels at either end of the skirt, continue in the Alternating Flat knot pattern. Leave aside the first 4 cords and work a row of 8 Flat knots.

Leave aside the first 6 cords and work a row of 7 Flat knots. Leave aside the first 8 cords and work a row of 6 Flat knots.

Continue in this way, ignoring a further 2 cords at the beginning of each row and working 1 less Flat knot in each row until you bring the section to a point with 1 Flat knot.

Repeat this pattern at the other end of the belt to make a corresponding triangle. You will now have 80 working cords across the centre. Now work the 2 triangles next to the outer ones – you work the centre one last.

Ignore the first 2 cords on either side and, working from each end, work a row of 5 Flat knots. Now continue in the Alternating Flat knot pattern and work a row of 4 knots, then 3 and so on, on each side, until you have brought both of these triangles to a point with 1 Flat knot. You will notice that these triangles get slightly smaller than the outer and centre ones.

To work the centre triangle begin with a row of 7 Flat knots and, working as already described, bring to a point with 1 Flat knot. Touch all knots on the edge of the work with a dab of clear adhesive to secure.

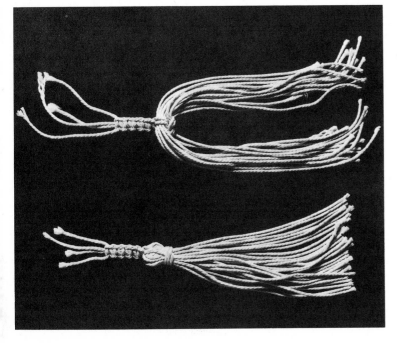

Full details for making the tassel ends of the ties are given overleaf. Each tassel is made up of 20 doubled cords and, when finished, is 8 inches long.

To make the sash ties

Cut 2 knotting cords, each 5yd long. Thread one cord through the last Lark's Head knot, to anchor it and, using the 2 holding cords and the added-on leader as centre cords, work a sennit of Flat knots 16in long.

Finish each end with a tassel. For each tassel, cut 20 extra cords, each 16in long, and tie all 4 ends of the sennit around them. Secure with coil wrapping (see photograph on page 78). This makes tassels 8in long.

To finish, trim all ends to the desired length, to give an even 'hemline' and finish each neatly with an Overhand knot.

Sailor's Belt

Change and change about – pick your buckle in silver, gilt or any colour to match the buttons on your dress or the clasps on your shoes. It's easy enough to make several belts in colours to match the outfits in your wardrobe, but quicker still to make just one and change the fastening.

Measurements

The belt is $1\frac{1}{2}$ in wide and 36in long. It is made to fit a waist measurement of about 27 to 32in, but the length can be adjusted to other requirements. There is no need to make holes for the prong – the Alternating Flat knot pattern leaves holes specially for the purpose!

Materials

64yd of No.18 cotton seine twine; 2 or more buckles with a bar $1\frac{1}{2}$ in long; for the working surface, a piece of board or an office clipboard; clear adhesive; pins.

Method

Divide the twine into 8 lengths. That is to say, cut 8 lengths each 8yd long. Mount the cords in the middle, either by pinning them to the board or securing them under the clip of a clipboard. Do not double the cords yet – mount them, so that you have only 8 knotting cords.

You begin working the belt in the centre of the loop.

1st row: Work 2 Flat knots.

2nd row: Ignore the first 2 cords, tie 1 Flat knot, leave last 2 cords.

3rd row: Work 2 Flat knots.

4th row: As 2nd row.

This is the Alternating Flat knot pattern used throughout the belt, except for the pattern blocks. Continue working in this pattern until you have 19 rows, ending with a 2-knot row. Now turn the work and continue the pattern in the other direction for the same distance. This completes the loop. Fold this narrow strip in half, bringing the ends together so that you have 16 working cords.

Continue in the Alternating Flat knot pattern. Now that you are working across the full width of the belt, you will have alternating rows of 4 knots and 3 knots respectively. Work in this way until the main section of the belt measures 9in, ending with a 3-knot row.

For the pattern block:

With the 4 left-hand cords, work 7 Flat knots. This is the sennit that forms the edging.

With cords 5, 6, 7 and 8 work a Spiral Twist of 14 Half knots. You will find that as you work this knot (which is, in effect, the first half of a Flat knot repeated) the work will twist of its own accord.

For the first spiral, always put the left-hand cord on top when working the Half knots. Reverse this process for the second spiral, working with the right-hand cord on top for each knot.

Repeat the spiral twist (right-hand cords on top) with cord 9, 10, 11 and 12. With cords 13, 14, 15 and 16, work a sennit of 7 Flat knots.

Now continue the Alternating Flat knot pattern for 15 rows, beginning and ending with a 3-knot row. Repeat the pattern block of Flat knot sennits and Half knot spiral twists as described above.

Work a further 15 rows of Alternating Flat knots. Repeat the pattern block. Now return to the Alternating Flat knot pattern for about 15in. You can adjust the length of the belt at this stage, working more or less rows to make it longer or shorter. Finish with a 3-knot row.

To finish the belt, leave aside the first and the last 4 cords and work a row of 2 Flat knots. Ignoring the first and last 6 cords, work 1 Flat knot, which should be in the middle so that the belt is shaped to a point at the end.

Using the left-hand cord as leader, work a row of Horizontal Double Half-Hitch cording down to the tip. Repeat with the right-hand cord as leader. Repeat these 2 steps, so that the belt is neatly finished, with 2 rows of cording at the tip.

Thread ends carefully out of sight at the back of the belt, taking the twine through about 3 or 4 knots in each case. Cut off ends and secure with a touch of colourless adhesive. Slip loop over buckle and thread end through.

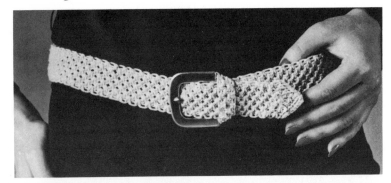

Josephine Knot Belt

Here's a belt that doesn't have a buckle – known as a sash belt. It is made of a continuing pattern of Josephine knots. They might look a little like a Chinese puzzle at first glance, but, like all macramé, are simple when you know how.

The belt shown on the right is worked in white twine only. But for clarity the knot is shown opposite in contrasting colours.

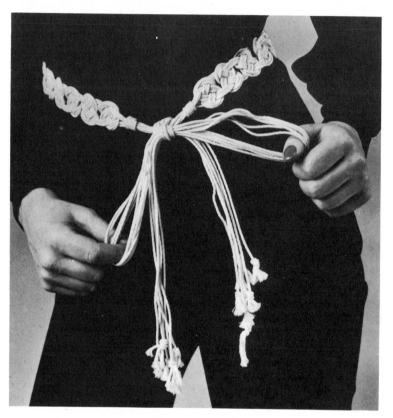

How to tie a Josephine Knot

The picture shows the knot worked with 2 strands each in contrasting colour, but for practice purposes it is simpler to work with single strands. Using different colours helps to identify them. Follow Figs. 32a, b, c, d and e closely until you can tie the knot easily. After that you are half-way to making the Josephine Knot belt.

To make a single knot, cut 2 lengths of cord each about 8in long, in dark and light colours. In our diagrams the light-coloured cord is referred to as cord A-B and the dark one, C-D.

Hold cord A-B in your left hand and make a loop in it (Fig. 32a), with end A on top of end B. Place cord C-D under the loop in the position shown in Fig. 32b. Take the lower end, D, and curve it over cord A-B, near the end A (Fig. 32c). Continuing with end D, pass it under cord A-B near the end B (Fig. 32d), diagonally over the loop, passing over cord A-B, under C-D and over A-B again (Fig. 32e).

In the photograph the knot has been left open so that you can follow the direction of the cords clearly, but in the belt, as you can see, it has been tightened so that it is just closed, to give a firmer fabric.

When the Josephine knot is used for a continuous pattern, the knots are alternately reversed. To tie the knot in the opposite direction, hold

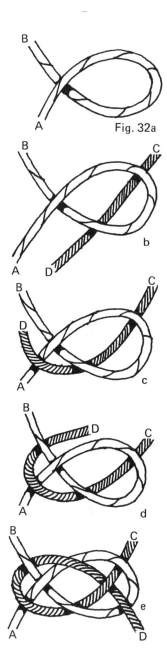

Fig. 32a

a mirror to the diagrams, Figs. a-e, and tie the knot in the back-to-front way you will see there, starting by making a loop in the right-hand cord, C-D, and weaving the left-hand cord, A-B, into it.

Measurements
The Josephine knot pattern is 26in long, plus a 22in fringe on each side for tying. Note that each Josephine knot is about 1in long, so that the length of the belt can be adjusted to any waist or hip measurement by working more or less knots.

Materials
30yd of thick (size 36) cotton or rayon seine twine (or stool twine); for the working surface, use a piece of board or foam block or an office clipboard; pins.

Method
Cut 6 lengths of twine, each 5yd long. These cords are used singly. Mount them at the middle of your chosen working surface. Pin cords individually to the block or foam, or secure to the clipboard. Holding 3 cords in each hand, tie 12 alternating Josephine knots. Make sure that the cords which lie on top, in one knot, are underneath in the next. This prevents the belt from twisting. Otherwise it will look like a spiral braid. Now turn the work and tie 12 more knots in the same way.

Finish with an Overhand knot or with a coil wrapping, as shown in the picture, at each end. Tie another Overhand knot about 4in along the fringe on each side. This holds the belt in place when loosely knotted. Trim the fringe to about 22in on each side and tie an Overhand knot at the end of each cord to prevent fraying.

Coloured Handbag

This is a simple, basic pattern for a handbag for which the twine is dyed at three stages in three dye colours. The fabric pattern of the bag has been chosen to be as unobtrusive as possible and to throw all emphasis on to the colour effect. Too many patterns, too many colours, and the look would be spoiled. However, the bag can, of course, be worked in natural twine or in a single colour. It is easy to vary the dimensions of the bag to make a satchel type to carry books and papers, a shopping or picnic holdall, or simply to lengthen the handle and make a shoulder bag. You might care to line the bag, if it is to hold small items.

Measurements
The bag measures 9in across and 11in in length, plus a 7in fringe; the handle is 22in long.

Materials
1lb ball of fillis garden twine, either 4 or 5-ply; 3 tins multi-purpose dye in related colours.

For the working surface, you can use heavy cardboard, a thin slab of polystyrene foam or an office clipboard. For the measurements given, a clipboard was ideal and the bag was knotted around that, no side seams being necessary. Choose or cut a working surface that is the correct width of the dimensions you require: the length is unimportant, since the bag can be moved up the surface as it is worked.

Method
Wash the twine in hot water and detergent and rinse thoroughly. Dye in lengths as already described. Cut 44 cords each 3yd long, which will give you 88 working cords.

Cut one cord 36in long and double it, to provide a strong holding cord.

If you wish to make a bag of a different width, add or subtract the cords in multiples of 8 to balance the work. Mount the 44 cords on to the doubled holding cord with Lark's Head knots. Tie the holding cord round the working surface.

To begin knotting: with each group of 4 cords, work 2 rows of Flat knots all round the working base, close to the holding cord.

Then, taking any 2 strings from 1 knot and 2 strings from the next knot (that is to say, starting anywhere round the width of the work), work 2 alternating rows of Flat knots all round.

This is the pattern. Repeat it until the bag is the desired length – in this case, 11in.

Remove the bag from the working surface and, holding the base of the bag towards you, take 2 cords from the front and 2 cords from the back (that is, those immediately behind one another) and tie a Flat knot.

This knot is not worked over a core, but is an ordinary reef (sometimes called a square) knot. Continue across the width of the bag, tying 2 front and 2 back cords together. This operation brings the edges together and forms the width of the bottom of the bag.

Now, working with the cords at the front, take 4 cords from the left-hand side and tie an Overhand knot close to the bottom of the bag. Continue all round the bag. For the last row of fringe, take 2 cords from one Overhand knot and 2 from the next, and tie another row of Overhand knots all round. Trim fringe to about 6in in length.

For the handle

Cut 2 54in lengths of the twine in any colour and mount with Lark's Head knots on to the holding cord at the top of the bag, between the groups of knots.

Now, using any short ends left from the bag, about 27 to 36in long, work Vertical Double Half-Hitch knots over cords, adding new knotting cords as needed. Secure each new cord with a pin while you are tying the first knot with it. Of course, if you wish, the handle can be worked with only one colour of twine, in which case there will be less ends to thread in.

When the handle is 22in long, or length desired, work 1 Double Half-Hitch over the holding cord at the other side of the bag, with all 4 knot leaders of the handle. Thread all ends into the back with a heavy wool needle.

Beads to Use with Macramé

Macramé and beads go together. As you can see from the door curtain in the colour picture facing page 37, the term 'beads' is used in the widest sense, to encompass any suitable cylindrical, oval or round object with a hole through it. The beads used on the sennit door curtain are short strips sawn from a natural bamboo cane, threaded at random along the Half knot spirals and Flat knot braids. Bought in a garden specialist shop in bundles intended for staking plants, they are an inexpensive way of decorating your work.

There is no end to the variety of beads you can use or make to accent your designs. The large wooden beads used on children's abacus counting frames and sold in toy-shops are ideal, especially the natural varnished wooden ones. You can also buy packets of beads in assorted sizes, shapes and colours in toy shops. Generally speaking, the rainbow profusion does not look well with macramé and it is better to sort the beads into different shapes of one colour, or into sets of toning colours, such as greens and browns, blues and mauves, and so on.

You can make beads from self-hardening modelling clay or garden clay fired in a kitchen boiler; from salt pastry baked rock hard; macaroni or other hollow pasta shapes; felt, coloured paper or magazine pictures rolled up, painted if necessary and varnished; stones or shells with natural holes, pierced acorns – practically anything, in fact. Naturally the size of the bead must relate to the scale of the work. Usually a bead will be carried on two knot-bearing cords, so it must have a hole large enough to take two thicknesses of the twine.

Here are a few ideas for beads you can make at home. For the best effects, if you paint the beads choose a colour as close as you can get to the twine you are using, or in a slightly lighter or darker shade of it. The contrast in texture – shiny bead, matt yarn – will be effective enough.

Modelling clay. Choose the kind that sets hard without firing. There are a number of different brands on the market – look for grey clay strengthened with nylon fibres. To make cylindrical beads, roll the clay into a long sausage shape and chop it up into the lengths you want. These need not be all the same length, even for use in the same piece of work. For oval beads, roll shorter sausage shapes and slightly pinch in the ends. For round beads, roll the clay between your palms into balls the size you need. Pierce the beads with a knitting needle or skewer and leave them in a warm place to set.

Another idea: roll out the clay into sheets about $\frac{3}{8}$ in thick and cut out circles, triangles, rectangles or other shapes. Imprint each shape with a pattern, using a small butter marker, a fancy button or a pastry decorator. Pierce two holes at the top of each disc and leave to dry. When set, paint the beads, leave them to dry and then varnish them to resemble ceramics. These flat disc beads can be used as 'charms' on a bracelet or as a pendant hanging on a thin macramé chain.

Garden Clay. Those who complain about having to garden on impossibly sticky clay soil might be pleased to find a use for it at last! Dig some clay, taking care not to include any lighter topsoil. Working on a surface well protected with newspaper and wearing rubber gloves, mould the clay in your fingers as described above into the shapes and size you want. Because clay naturally shrinks as it dries, it is a good idea to pierce the long sausage shapes or thread the balls on to a steel knitting needle or skewer and leave them in place until the clay has set.

Put the clay in the fire box of a domestic boiler or solid-fuel cooker when it is cold and before you light the fire. Fire the clay overnight. Do not put the clay into a hot oven or in the fire box with the fire already alight, or it might explode.

When the beads are cold, paint them with acrylic paint. The beads will dry in slightly varying shades of the colour, which adds interest.

Felt. For each bead cut a strip of felt 9in long and 1in wide. Taper each long side so that ends meet in a point. Fold over wide end $\frac{1}{2}$in. Holding fold down, dab adhesive lightly along centre of strip to narrow end. Roll strip lightly over a knitting needle from wide end to narrow end. Secure with a dab of adhesive. This will give you an oval bead approximately $\frac{3}{4}$in long.

Paper. Much the same technique can be used to make paper beads. Again, cut a paper strip 9in by 1in. Taper the sides to a pointed triangle. Roll the strip round a fine knitting needle so that the bead is tightly and evenly coiled. When you come to the last 2in, dab the paper with glue and then complete the rolling. Hold the bead between your fingers for a few moments until the glue has dried. You can make beads of this type with newspaper and then paint them with poster paints, with strong, plain-coloured paper or even, for a mottled effect, in paper cut from magazine pictures.

To make cylindrical beads, cut 9in strips of paper with straight sides. The width of each strip governs the length of each bead. Tightly wrap the strip of paper round a knitting needle, remembering to choose one that will leave a large-enough hole in the bead. Dab adhesive on to the last inch or two as you roll. Paint the beads and, for extra strength, varnish them when they are dry.

Pasta. Beads made from pasta shapes such as macaroni are naturally rather fragile and suitable only for articles that will not come under any strain or pressure. Do not use them, therefore, around the fringe of a waistcoat or on a beaded curtain that will constantly be pushed out of the way. They are ideal, however, on items such as wallhangings or even window curtains. You can leave the pasta in its natural creamy colourings, which usually will tone well with the undyed colour of your twine, or paint the shapes with powder colours to tone with the colour you are using.

Salt pastry. Hard as rock and just as inedible, salt pastry makes a wonderfully durable material for decorative beads. Here is the recipe:

Ingredients. You will need 4 cups of plain flour, one cup of salt and $1\frac{1}{2}$ cups of water.

Mix the flour and salt together and gradually add the water, mixing until you have a pliable dough that will hold its shape. Do not let it become sticky. The precise amount of water you will need will depend on the quality and absorbency of the flour – this is why you must add it gradually. Knead the dough well. Shape the dough into sausage shapes and cut into short lengths, ovals, balls or discs, whatever you like. Thread the beads on to metal skewers, and pierce holes in discs. Push out holes slightly larger than you need because they will shrink when the pastry is baked.

Place the shapes on a baking tray and bake at 325deg F, Gas Mark 3, for about $1\frac{1}{2}$ hours, until the pastry is completely dried out and hard. Remove from oven and allow to cool thoroughly. Paint with acrylic or poster colours, and when dry varnish with matt varnish.

Natural materials. There is an easy affinity between macramé worked with natural twines and beads made of natural materials. If you are a beachcomber by instinct, you might already have an interesting collection of items just waiting to be used in this way. Stones with natural holes are ideal companions to a piece of macramé. You will probably not have many of these, so reserve them for a design that needs the accent of just a few beads.

Shells with holes are ideal, too, and can be threaded on fine macramé chains to make fun gypsy-type jewellery. Although it is quite possible to drill holes in stones and shells, they somehow never seem as satisfying as those you have found with a hole worn away by years of pounding tides! Acorns can be pierced and varnished; here the warm woody colour of the nut blends well with natural twines.

Lastly, look out for beads in boxes at jumble sales. Often a broken necklace is eventually given away by someone who has never got round to re-threading it; sometimes boxes of old buttons will disclose perfect bead material. And, of course, there are your friends. Choose the ones who are always begging bits and pieces from you for their patch-work project or for dolls' clothes, and ask them to do you a favour in return!

The Cavandoli Technique

There is a close similarity between some types of macramé and needle-craft, most evident in the macramé form known as Cavandoli. Although this technique is worked solely with knots, it has the appearance of needlework.

The technique is not at all difficult to master, since it only uses one knot, the Double Half-Hitch. This is worked as horizontal cording in the background colour and vertical cording in the pattern colour.

The threads in the background colour – blue in our sampler – are set on to the holding cord, or dowel, and travel downwards through the work, coming to the surface only when they are used for the cording. The pattern colour – red here – is used as leader for the rows of horizontal cording. This colour is revealed only when it forms the Vertical Double Half-Hitches that make the pattern.

Designs in this type of work are traditionally geometric, and can be worked out on graph paper. Indeed, designs for tapestry, cross-stitch and rug-making are readily adapted to Cavandoli work. Normally only two colours are used, but the wallhanging with Turkish motifs we chose as an example does, in fact, have three – the Air Force blue of the background, two shades of red for the pattern colour, to give the work the faded appearance of age, plus black for the edging.

Designs of this kind are suitable for braids, bookmarks, headbands, chokers, wristbands or watch straps, belts and cushions.

It is important to choose a strong, smooth-running thread for this work. Fine string, smooth crochet and knitting yarns, and rug wool are all suitable. When calculating the length of yarn you will need, allow at least eight times the length of the finished work for the background, set-on, threads. You will need almost exactly the same amount of the pattern colour – that is, the sum total of all the background threads.

When working out or adapting designs for Cavandoli knotting, one factor must be borne in mind. Each square of the design represents one knot, but in the case of the background colour, the knots are Horizontal Double Half-Hitches, worked one beside the other, whereas in the case of the pattern colour each square represents Vertical Double Half-Hitch, where the knots are worked one above the other. You must be prepared, therefore, for the design to be more elongated than its representation on graph paper would appear.

Measurements
The wallhanging is 5in wide by 29in long, including the 9in coil-wrapped fringe.

Materials
An 8in long piece of $\frac{1}{4}$in dowel; a total of approximately 5oz rug wool. You can choose colours from the maker's range or, as we did, dye

blue

black

red

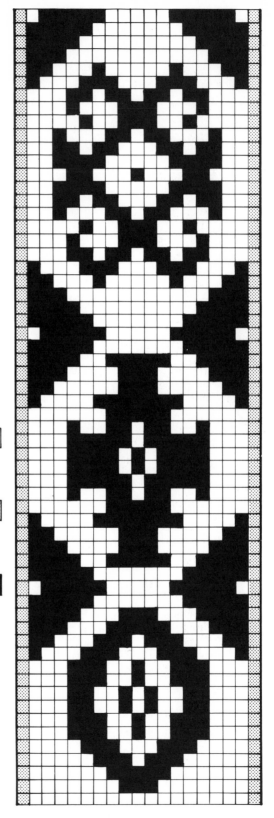

natural-coloured wool with commercial dyes. We achieved a soft blue grey by using a mid blue to which a little black was added; the red with a red/orange mixture and the addition of a little black; and a muted black. Multi-purpose dyes were used and the wool simmered for only a short time, so that the strength of the colours was below normal. To give the mottled, two-tone effect to the red, it was dyed unevenly; some of it was left out of the dye bath for part of the time.

The hanging as shown uses the following quantities: Blue wool, 9 lengths, each 8yd long; black wool, 8yd length; red wool, 20yd, used in 2 or more pieces for ease of knotting.

Method

Mount 9 blue cords on the dowel with Lark's Head knots – giving 18 working cords. Lay the centre of the black cord on top of the blue cords, just below the dowel, pin it out on the left-hand side and work a row of Horizontal Double Half-Hitch cording over it, close to the Lark's Head knots. The black cords now become knotting cords at both ends.

Take the left-hand blue cord and pin out of the way. This design demands an uneven number of knotting cords, and the extra cord will become the means of hanging the piece.

Take a piece of red wool about 4 or 5yd long – the length is immaterial, as a new length can be added later within a row of cording. Lay it over all 19 working cords and knot a row of Horizontal Double Half-Hitch over it – you will have a black knot at either end.

Next row: Using the same red knot bearer, work 1 black knot and 7 blue knots in Horizontal Double Half-Hitch. Lay the next blue cord on top of the red, and make a Vertical Double Half-Hitch with the red. Do the same with the next 2 blue cords and then revert to Horizontal Double Half-Hitch – blue over the red knot bearer and a black knot at the end.

Now you can proceed with the hanging by following the chart – each square represents one knot.

When the red knot bearer (which is used up very quickly when it becomes the knotting cord) runs short, add a new length alongside it inside a row of blue cording. Knot over both for a few stitches and then continue with the new cord. Trim away when work is complete.

To finish:

Cut the knotting cords to an even length – about 12in – and divide into five groups (one group will be 1 cord short, but this is not important). Lay hanging with work to the right and fringe to the left and cut 5 lengths of red wool, about 1yd each.

Work coil wrapping around each group, as follows: Lay a 3in loop of red on the first group of blue cords – loop to the left and an end long enough to pull easily extending up the hanging. Now take the long red end and start winding firmly from the hanging end about 2in down the fringe. Slip red end through the red loop – which should show beyond the winding – and pull the other red end firmly (see photograph 5). This links the ends and pulls them up inside the wrapping. Clip ends. Repeat on the other groups – trim blue fringe to 7in below the wrapping and fray out ends of blue and black cords.

For the hanging cord: Bring extra blue cords to the other end of dowel, leaving a 15in loop, for hanging. Wind end round dowel one stitch from end, to keep it from slipping off, and thread end through knots at the back to secure.

Wrapping a coil. This technique is used to finish the ends of the Cavandoli wallhanging described on this page.

Index

746.7
G543r

c-1

PJo

Gladwin, Noreen.
Rugmaking &
guide / Noreen & macrame
London : Noreen Gladwin
79 p. : Hamlyn Gladwin
Includes ill. [c1974
index. (some co

1. Rugs. 2. Macramé.
joint author. II. Title

JOCCxc

746.7
G543r   Gladwin, Noreen.
            Rugmaking & macrame : a step-by-step
          guide / Noreen Gladwin and Anna North.
          London : Hamlyn, [c1974].
            79 p. : ill. (some col.) ; 26 cm.
            Includes index.

c-1   CAMBRIA COUNTY LIBRARY
                    Johnstown, Pa 15901

                      FINES PER DAY:
                  Adults 5¢, Children 2¢

          1. Rugs. 2. Macramé. I. North, Anna,
        joint author. II. Title

PJo   JOCCxc